THE FORMULA OF THE INSTITUTE:
NOTES FOR A COMMENTARY

The Constitutions of the Society of Jesus

THE FORMULA OF THE INSTITUTE

Notes for a Commentary

by

Antonio M. de Aldama, S.J.

Translated by
Ignacio Echániz, S.J.

ROME
Centrum Ignatianum Spiritualitatis

ST. LOUIS
The Institute of Jesuit Sources

This book is an authorized translation of *Notas para un comentario a la Fórmula del Instituto de la Compañía de Jesús* by Antonio M. de Aldama, S.J., 1981, published by Centrum Ignatianum Spiritualitis, Borgo S. Spirito 5, 00195 Rome, Italy.

First Edition
distributed in the Americas, Australia, and New Zealand
by the Institute of Jesuit Sources,
and in Europe
by Centrum Ignatianum Spiritualitatis.

Note: There is another edition, authorized for
sale only in Asia and Africa, which can be
ordered from Gujarat Sahitya Prakash,
Anand 388 001, India.

ISBN 0-912422-55-6 Hardcover
ISBN 0-912422-56-4 Paperback

CONTENTS

FOREWORD ix

ABBREVIATIONS x

THE TEXTS OF THE 1539 "FIVE CHAPTERS" AND OF THE
1550 FORMULA OF THE INSTITUTE 1

INTRODUCTION: HISTORY AND SIGNIFICANCE OF
THE FORMULA 25
    I. ORIGIN AND EVOLUTION 25
        1. The First Draft 28
        2. The Second Draft 30
        3. The Third Draft 31
    II. SIGNIFICANCE OF THE FORMULA 33

THE FIRST CHAPTER: THE AIM OF THE SOCIETY
AND ITS INSTITUTIONALIZATION 39
    I. THE AIM OF THE SOCIETY 39
        Note: Structure of the Text 39
        1. The Subject 39
        2. The Aims and Specific Means 40
            a. The Aims 41
            b. Specific Means 42
            c. The Three Adverbs 44
        3. Secondary Activities 44
        4. Gratuity 45
        5. Exhortation 46
            a. Reflection 46
            b. Recommendation 47
    II. INSTITUTIONALIZATION 47
        1. The Superior 48
        2. The Legislation 50
        3. The Council 51
            a. Matters of Major Importance 51
            b. Matters of Lesser Importance 53

THE SECOND CHAPTER: THE VOW OF OBEDIENCE TO THE POPE 55

   I. THE VOW 55

      1. The Spirit of the Vow 55

      2. Reasons for Taking the Vow 57

      3. Modality of the Vow 58

         a. Who Make the Vow 58

         b. It Is a Special Vow 58

         c. The Object of the Vow 59

   II. OBSERVANCE OF THE VOW 61

      1. Reflection 61

      2. Availability 62

      3. Indifference 63

THE THIRD CHAPTER: THE VOW OF OBEDIENCE TO THE SUPERIOR OF THE SOCIETY 67

   I. THE VOW 67

   II. ELECTION AND AUTHORITY OF THE SUPERIOR GENERAL 68

      1. Election 68

      2. Authority 69

   III. HOW TO EXERCISE AUTHORITY AND PRACTICE OBEDIENCE 69

      1. How to Exercise Authority 69

         a. What He Should Command 69

         b. How He Should Command 70

      2. Recommendation on the Teaching of Catechism 71

      3. How to Practice Obedience 72

THE FOURTH CHAPTER: THE VOW OF POVERTY 75

   I. THE POVERTY OF THE SOCIETY 75

      1. The Reasons 75

      2. The Poverty of the Society in F39 and F40 77

      3. Vacillations as regards this Poverty 79

      4. The Poverty of the Society in F50 81

   II. THE EXCEPTION IN THE CASE OF THE SCHOLASTICS 83

      1. The Purpose of the Colleges 83

      2. Administrative Setup of the Colleges 84

         a. Establishment of the Colleges 85

         b. Superintendency by the Society 87

         c. Advantages of this System 87

      3. The Students of the Colleges 88

THE FIFTH CHAPTER: TWO JESUIT PECULIARITIES 91

    I. CHOIR 91

    II. COMMON LIFE IN MATTERS EXTERNAL 92

THE CONCLUDING REMARKS 95

    I. PURPOSE OF THE FORMULA 95

    II. CAUTION IN ADMITTING TO PROFESSION 96

    III. THE COADJUTORS 98

        1. Fitness 99

        2. The Vows 100

    IV. PRAYER AND DOXOLOGY 101

FINAL REFLECTIONS 103

    I. A PRIESTLY RELIGIOUS ORDER 103

    II. AN APOSTOLIC ORDER 104

    III. AN ORDER UNITED BY A SPECIAL BOND TO THE POPE 105

INDEX OF NAMES 107

FOREWORD

These notes had been written for a series of talks on the Formula of the Institute. Someone happened to see them and encouraged me to publish them. I agreed because of the scarcity of such studies, even though the Formula—as GC 31 declared—occupies pride of place in our Institute.

They focus on the draft approved by Julius III on July 21, 1550, the one that reflects Ignatius' final thinking, but they also indicate the differences between this final draft and its two predecessors of 1539 and 1540.

The notes are preceded by the text of the Formula divided into five chapters and a conclusion. This was its original form, changed in the bulls of approval to suit the *stylus curiae*. The division into nine numbers came later. This, too, has been kept; though it is arbitrary, it is often used in the Society's official documents.

My only desire is that these notes—an exegetical commentary on the Formula—may be followed by other studies from various points of view: historical, juridical, spiritual, theological, biblical . . . *Faxit Deus!*

ABBREVIATIONS

AHSI	*Archivum Historicum Societatis Iesu*
Autobiog	The *Autobiography* of St. Ignatius
GC	General Congregation
CIC	*Codex Iuris Canonici* (1917)
CIS	Centrum Ignatianum Spiritualitatis
Const	Constitutions of the Society of Jesus
Exam	General Examen
F39	Formula of the Institute orally approved in 1539 by Paul III (MI Const I 16-20)
F40	Formula of the Institute approved in 1540 by Paul III in the bull *Regimini* (MI Const I 26-30)
F50	Formula of the Institute approved in 1550 by Julius III in the bull *Exposcit* (MI Const I 375-381)
MHSI Nadal	Monumenta Historica Societatis Iesu. *Epistolae P. Hieronymi Nadal.* 6 vols.
MI	Monumenta Ignatiana
Const	*Constitutiones et Regulae Societatis Iesu.* 4 vols.
Epp	*S. Ignatii Epistolae et Instructiones.* 12 vols.
FontDoc	*Fontes Documentales de S. Ignatio*
FontNarr	*Fontes Narrativi de S. Ignatio.* 2 vols.
SpEx	Exercitia Spiritualia. The *Spiritual Exercises* of St. Ignatius
Young	William J. Young, S.J., trans. *Letters of St. Ignatius of Loyola.* Chicago: Loyola University Press, 1959.

THE TEXTS OF THE "FIVE CHAPTERS" OF 1539
AND OF
THE FORMULA OF THE INSTITUTE OF 1550

On the even-numbered pages which follow is the text of the "Five Chapters" of 1539. This venerable text is the very first foundational document, candidly stating the principal points of the new institute. The original Latin text is found in MI Const I 16-20.

Facing this text on the odd-numbered pages is the Formula of the Institute of 1550. This is the revised text of the Formula in which some points are restated or developed to meet the requirements of the Roman Curia. The original Latin is found in MI Const I 375-381.

1539 "FIVE CHAPTERS"

CHAPTER 1

Whoever desires to serve as a soldier of God
beneath the banner of the cross in our Society,
which we desire to be designated by the name of Jesus,
and to serve the Lord alone
and His vicar on earth,
should,
after a solemn vow of perpetual chastity,
keep what follows in mind.

He is a member of a community founded chiefly for this purpose:
to strive especially
for the progress of souls in Christian life and doctrine
and for the propagation of the faith
by the ministry of the word,
by Spiritual Exercises,
by works of charity,
and expressly by the education of children
and unlettered persons in Christianity.

1550 FORMULA OF THE INSTITUTE

CHAPTER 1

[1]

Whoever desires to serve as a soldier of God
beneath the banner of the cross in our Society,
which we desire to be designated by the name of Jesus,
and to serve the Lord alone
and the Church, His spouse,
under the Roman pontiff, the vicar of Christ on earth,
should,
after a solemn vow of perpetual chastity, poverty, and obedience,
keep what follows in mind

He is a member of a Society founded chiefly for this purpose:
to strive especially
for the defense and propagation of the faith
and for the progress of souls in Christian life and doctrine,
by means of public preaching, lectures,
and any other ministration whatsoever of the word of God,
and further by means of the Spiritual Exercises,
the education of children and unlettered persons
in Christianity,
and the spiritual consolation of Christ's faithful
through hearing confessions
and administering the other sacraments.

Moreover, he should show himself ready
to reconcile the estranged,
compassionately assist and serve those in prisons or hospitals,
and indeed to perform any other works of charity,
according to what will seem expedient
for the glory of God and the common good.

Furthermore, all these works should be carried out
altogether free of charge

Still further, let any such person take care
to keep always before his eyes first God,
and then the nature of this Institute
which is, so to speak, a pathway to God;
and then let him strive with all his effort
to achieve this end set before him by God—
each one, however,
according to the grace which the Holy Spirit has given to him
and according to the particular grade of his own vocation,
lest anyone should perhaps show zeal,
but a zeal which is not according to knowledge.

The decision about each one's grade
and the selection and entire distribution of employments
shall be in the power of the superior general
or ordinary who is to be elected by us,
in order that the proper order
necessary in every well-organized community
may be preserved.

This superior general,
with the advice of the brethren,
shall possess the authority, in council
(a majority of votes always having the right to decide),
to draw up constitutions
leading to the achievement of this end
which has been proposed to us.

and without accepting any remuneration
for the labor expended in all the aforementioned activities.

Still further, let any such person take care,
as long as he lives,
first of all to keep before his eyes God
and then the nature of this Institute
which is, so to speak, a pathway to God;
and then let him strive with all his effort
to achieve this end set before him by God—
each one, however,
according to the grace which the Holy Spirit has given to him
and according to the particular grade of his own vocation.

[2]

Consequently, lest anyone should perhaps show zeal,
but a zeal which is not according to knowledge,
the decision about each one's grade
and the selection and entire distribution of employments
shall be in the power of the superior general
or ordinary who at any future time is to be elected by us,
or in the power of those whom this superior general
may appoint under himself with that authority,
in order that the proper order
necessary in every well-organized community
may be preserved.

This superior general,
with the council of his associates
(with the majority of votes always having the right to prevail),
shall possess the authority to compose constitutions
leading to the achievement of this end
which has been proposed to us.
He shall also have the authority
to explain officially doubts which may arise
in connection with our Institute as comprised in this Formula.

In matters that are more serious and lasting,
the council should be understood to be
the greater part of the whole Society
which can conveniently be summoned
by the superior general;

in lighter and more temporary matters
it will be all those who happen to be present
in the place where our superior resides.
All right to execute and command, however,
will be in the power of the superior.

CHAPTER 2

All the companions should know
and daily bear in mind,
not only when they first make their profession
but as long as they live,
that this entire Society and each one individually
are campaigning for God
under faithful obedience to His Holiness Paul III
and are thus under the command of the vicar of Christ
and his divine power
not only because we are bound
by the obligation common to all clerics,
but also by the vow we make
to carry out
without subterfuge or excuse

The council, which must necessarily be convoked
to establish or change the Constitutions
and for other matters of more than ordinary importance,
such as the alienation or dissolution
of houses and colleges once erected,
should be understood
(according to the explanation in our Constitutions)
to be the greater part of the entire professed Society
which can be summoned without grave inconvenience
by the superior general.

In other matters which are of lesser importance,
the same general,
aided by counsel from his brethren
to the extent that he will deem fitting,
shall have the full right personally to order and command
whatever he judges in the Lord
to pertain to the glory of God and the common good,
as will be explained in the Constitutions.

CHAPTER 2

[3]

All who make the profession in this Society
should understand at the time,
and furthermore keep in mind as long as they live,
that this entire Society
and the individual members who make their profession in it
are campaigning for God
under faithful obedience to His Holiness Pope Paul III
and his successors in the Roman pontificate.

The Gospel does indeed teach us,
and we know from orthodox faith and firmly hold,
that all of Christ's faithful
are subject to the Roman pontiff as their head

and at once (as far as in us lies)
whatever His Holiness may order
pertaining to the progress of souls
and the propagation of the faith,
whether he decides to send us among the Turks,
or to the New World,
or to the Lutherans,
or to any others whether infidels or faithful.

Therefore, before those who will come to us
take this burden upon their shoulders,
they should ponder long and seriously,
as the Lord has counseled,
whether they possess among their resources
enough spiritual capital to complete this tower;
that is, whether the Holy Spirit who moves them
is offering them so much grace that with His aid
they have hope of bearing the weight of this vocation.
Then, after they have enlisted
through the inspiration of the Lord
in this militia of Christ,
they ought to be prompt in carrying out
this obligation which is so great,
being clad for battle day and night.

and as the vicar of Christ.
Yet for the sake of greater devotion
in obedience to the Apostolic See,
of greater abnegation of our own wills,
and of surer direction from the Holy Spirit,
we have judged it to be extremely profitable
if each one of us
and all those who may make the same profession in the future
would, in addition to the ordinary bond of the three vows,
be bound by a special vow to carry out,
without subterfuge or excuse
and at once (as far as in us lies),
whatever the present and future Roman pontiffs may order
pertaining to the progress of souls
and the propagation of the faith,
and to go to whatsoever provinces
they may choose to send us,
whether they decide to send us among the Turks
or any other infidels,
even those who live in the regions called the Indies,
or among any heretics or schismatics
or any of the faithful.

[4]

Therefore before those who will come to us
take this burden upon their shoulders,
they should ponder long and seriously,
as the Lord has counseled,
whether they possess among their resources
enough spiritual capital to complete this tower;
that is, whether the Holy Spirit who moves them
is offering them so much grace that with His aid
they have hope of bearing the weight of this vocation.
Then, after they have enlisted
through the inspiration of the Lord
in this militia of Christ,
they ought to be prompt in carrying out
this obligation which is so great,
being clad for battle day and night.

However, to forestall among us any ambition
for such missions or provinces,
or any refusal of them,
let each one promise
never to carry on negotiations with the Roman pontiff
about such missions
directly or indirectly,
but leave all this care to God
and to His vicar
and to the superior of the Society.
This superior, too, just like the rest,
shall also promise not to approach the pontiff at all
either one way or another
concerning a mission of his own,
except with the advice of the Society.

CHAPTER 3

All should likewise vow that
in all matters that concern the observance of this Rule
they will be obedient to the one put in charge of the Society.

The latter, however, should issue
the commands which he knows to be opportune
for achieving the end set before him
by God and the Society.

[5]

However, to forestall among us any ambition
for such missions or provinces,
or any refusal of them,
all our members should have this understanding:
they should not
either by themselves or through someone else
carry on negotiations with the Roman pontiff
about such missions,
but leave all this care to God,
and to the pope himself as His vicar,
and to the superior general of the Society.
Indeed, the general too, just like the rest,
should not treat with the said pontiff
about himself being sent or not,
unless after advice from the Society.

CHAPTER 3

|6|

All should likewise vow that
in all matters that concern the observance of this Rule
they will be obedient to the one put in charge of the Society.
He should be the best qualified for this office
and will be elected by a majority of votes
(as will be explained in the Constitutions).
He should possess all the authority and power
over the Society which are useful
for its good administration, correction, and government.

He should issue the commands which he knows
to be opportune for achieving the end
set before him by God and the Society.

In his superiorship he should be ever mindful
of the kindness, meekness, and charity of Christ
and of the pattern set by Peter and Paul,
a norm which both he and the council
should keep constantly in view.
Particularly let them hold esteemed
the instruction of children and the unlettered
in the Christian doctrine of the Ten Commandments
and other similar rudiments, whatever will seem suitable
to them in accordance with the circumstances
of persons, places, and times.
For it is very necessary that the superior and the council
give this matter the most diligent attention
since the edifice of faith cannot arise
among our fellowmen without a foundation,
and since there is the danger that
as one becomes more learned
he may disregard this occupation,
less prestigious at first glance,
when none in fact is more fruitful
either for the neighbor to be edified
or for Ours to discharge occupations
that combine both humility and charity.
Assuredly, too, the subjects,
both because of the great value of good order
and for the sake of the constant practice
of humility, never sufficiently praised,
should always be obliged to obey the general
in all matters pertaining to the Society's Institute
and to recognize and properly venerate
Christ as present in him.

CHAPTER 4

From experience we have learned
that a life removed as far as possible
from all contagion of avarice
and as like as possible to evangelical poverty

In his superiorship he should be ever mindful
of the kindness, meekness, and charity of Christ
and of the pattern set by Peter and Paul,
a norm which both he and the aforementioned council
should keep constantly in view.
Assuredly, too,
because of the great value of good order
and for the sake of the constant practice
of humility, never sufficiently praised,
the individual subjects should not only be obliged
to obey the general
in all matters pertaining to the Society's Institute
but also to recognize and properly venerate
Christ as present in him.

CHAPTER 4

[7]

From experience we have learned
that a life removed as far as possible
from all contagion of avarice
and as like as possible to evangelical poverty

is more gratifying, more undefiled,
and more suitable for the edification of our fellowmen.
We likewise know that our Lord Jesus Christ
will supply to His servants
who are seeking only the kingdom of God
what is necessary for food and clothing.

Therefore our members, one and all,
should vow perpetual poverty,
declaring that they cannot,
either individually or in common,
acquire any civil right
to any stable goods
or any produce or fixed income
for the maintenance or use of the Society.
Rather let them be content to enjoy only
the use of necessary things,
with the owners permitting,
and to receive the money and the value of things given them
in order to buy necessities for themselves.

They may, however, acquire the civil right
to stable goods and to fixed income
in order to bring together some talented students
and instruct them, especially in sacred letters,
in the universities,
that is, for the support of those students
who desire to advance in the spirit and in letters
and at length to be received into our Society
after probation
when the period of their studies has been finished.

is more gratifying, more undefiled,
and more suitable for the edification of our fellowmen.
We likewise know that our Lord Jesus Christ
will supply to His servants
who are seeking only the kingdom of God
what is necessary for food and clothing.

Therefore our members, one and all,
should vow perpetual poverty in such a manner
that neither the professed,
either individually or in common,
nor any house or church of theirs
can acquire any civil right to any produce,
fixed revenues, or possessions
or to the retention of any stable goods
(except those which are proper for their own use and habitation);
but they should instead be content
with whatever is given them out of charity
for the necessities of life.

[8]

However, the houses which the Lord will provide
are to be dedicated to labor in His vineyard
and not to the pursuit of scholastic studies;
and on the other hand it appears altogether proper
that workers should be provided for that same vineyard
from among the young men who are inclined to piety
and capable of applying themselves to learning,
in order that they may be a kind of seminary
for the Society, including the professed Society.

Consequently, to provide facilities for studies,
the professed Society should be capable
of having colleges of scholastics
wherever benefactors will be moved by their devotion
to build and endow them.

We now petition that as soon as these colleges
will have been built and endowed
(but not from resources
which it pertains to the Holy See to apply),
they may be established through authorization of the Holy See
or considered to be so established.
These colleges should be capable of possessing
fixed revenues, rights to rentals, or possessions
which are to be applied to the uses and needs of the students.

The general of the Society retains
the full government or superintendency
over the aforementioned colleges and students;
and this pertains
to the choice of rectors or governors
and of the scholastics;
the admission, dismissal, reception, and exclusion of the same;
the enactment of statutes;
the arrangement, instruction, edification,
and correction of the scholastics;
the manner of supplying them with food, clothing,
and all other necessary materials;
and every other kind of government, control, and care

All this should be managed in such a way that
neither may the students be able
to abuse the aforementioned goods
nor may the professed Society be able
to convert them to its own uses,
but may use them to provide for the needs of the scholastics.

These students, moreover, should have
such intellectual ability and moral character
as to give solid hope
that they will be suitable for the Society's functions
after their studies are completed,
and that thus at length,
after their progress in spirit and learning

CHAPTER 5

All the members who are in holy orders,
even though they can acquire no right
to benefices and revenues,
should nonetheless be obliged to recite the office
according to the rite of the Church,
but not in choir lest they be diverted
from the works of charity to which
we have fully dedicated ourselves.
Hence too they should use neither organs nor singing
in their Masses and other religious ceremonies;
for these laudably enhance the divine worship
of other clerics and religious
and have been found to arouse and move souls,
by bringing them into harmony with the hymns and rites,
but we have experienced them to be
a considerable hindrance to us, since
according to the nature of our vocation,
besides the other necessary duties,
we must frequently be engaged
a great part of the day and even of the night
in comforting the sick both in body and in spirit.

CONCLUSION

These are the matters which we have been able to explain
about our profession in a kind of sketch,
which we now do in order to give brief information
both to those who ask us about our plan of life
and also to those who will later on follow us
if, God willing, we shall ever have imitators along this path.

has become manifest
and after sufficient testing,
they can be admitted into our Society.

CHAPTER 5

Since all the members should be priests,
they should be obliged to recite the Divine Office
according to the ordinary rite of the Church,
but privately and not in common or in choir.

Also, in what pertains to food, clothing,
and other external things,
they will follow the common and approved usage
of reputable priests,
so that if anything is subtracted in this regard
in accordance with each one's need
or desire of spiritual progress,
it may be offered, as will be fitting,
out of devotion and not obligation,
as a reasonable service of the body to God.

CONCLUSION

[9]

These are the matters which we were able to explain
about our profession in a kind of sketch,
through the good pleasure of our previously mentioned
sovereign pontiff Paul and of the Apostolic See.
We have now completed this explanation,
in order to give brief information
both to those who ask us about our plan of life

By experience we have learned that
the path has many and great difficulties
connected with it.
Consequently we have judged it opportune
to admonish those not to fall,
under the appearance of good,
into these two things we have avoided.
One is not to impose on the companions
under pain of mortal sin
any fasts, disciplines, baring of feet or head,
color of dress, type of food, penances, hairshirts,
and other torments of the flesh.
These, however, we do not prohibit
because we condemn them,
for we greatly praise and approve them
in those who observe them;
but only because we do not wish Ours
either to be crushed by so many burdens together
or to allege any excuse for not carrying out
what we have set before ourselves.
But everyone can exercise himself devoutly
in the practices he deems to be necessary
or useful for himself,
provided the superior does not forbid him.
The other is that no one be received into the Society
unless he has first been tested
for a long time and very diligently;
and only when he appears prudent in Christ
and conspicuous either in learning or in holiness of life
may he be admitted into the militia of Jesus Christ.

and also to those who will later follow us
if, God willing, we shall ever have imitators along this path.

By experience we have learned that
the path has many and great difficulties
connected with it.

Consequently we have judged it opportune
to decree that no one should be permitted
to pronounce his profession in this Society
unless his life and doctrine have been probed
by long and exacting tests
(as will be explained in the Constitutions).
For in all truth this Institute requires men
who are thoroughly humble and prudent in Christ
as well as conspicuous in the integrity
of Christian life and learning.

May Christ deign to be favorable
to these our tender beginnings,
to the glory of God the Father,
to whom alone be glory and honor forever.
Amen.

Moreover, some persons will be admitted
to become coadjutors either for spiritual
or temporal concerns
or to become scholastics.
After sufficient probations
and the time specified in the Constitutions,
these too should,
for their greater devotion and merit,
pronounce their vows.
But their vows will not be solemn
(except in the case of some who
with permission from the superior general
will be able to make three solemn vows of this kind
because of their devotion and personal worth).
Instead, they will be vows by which these persons
are bound as long as the superior general
thinks that they should be retained in the Society,
as will be explained more fully in the Constitutions.
But these coadjutors and scholastics too
should be admitted into this militia of Jesus Christ
only after they have been diligently examined
and found suitable for that same end of the Society.

And may Christ deign to be favorable
to these our tender beginnings,
to the glory of God the Father,
to whom alone be glory and honor forever.
Amen.

INTRODUCTION:
HISTORY AND SIGNIFICANCE OF THE FORMULA

I. ORIGIN AND EVOLUTION

In a talk he gave on the origins of the Society when he visited the scholastics of Alcalá and Salamanca in February-March 1554, Fr. Nadal told them, among other things, that our Lord helped St. Ignatius to write the Spiritual Exercises while he was at Manresa, "so leading him that he would devote himself entirely to his service and the aid of souls; he showed him this with devotion, particularly in two exercises, those of the King and the Standards. That is where Ignatius understood his goal, the aim he should pursue in his every undertaking, and that is now the aim of the Society."[1]

This testimony of one of his closest associates shows us how we can trace the first origins of the Formula of the Institute. "Particularly in two exercises, those of the King and the Standards . . . Ignatius understood his goal, the aim he should pursue . . . , and that is now the aim of the Society."

The composition of place for the meditation of the King or the Kingdom ("the synagogues, villages, and towns where Christ our Lord preached")—an implicit quotation of the last verses of Matthew 9—suggests the true setting: Jesus' own evangelical journeys and the mission of the Apostles:

> "Jesus made a tour through all the towns and villages, teaching in their synagogues, proclaiming the Good News of the kingdom and curing all kinds of diseases and sickness. And when he saw the crowds, he felt sorry for them because they were harassed and dejected like sheep without a shepherd. . . . He summoned his twelve disciples and gave them authority over unclean spirits. . . . These twelve Jesus sent out, instructing them as follows: 'Proclaim that the kingdom of heaven is close at hand. Cure the sick, raise the dead, cleanse the lepers, cast out devils. You received

1 MHSI Nadal V 40.

without charge, give without charge. . . .' "[2]

The meditation itself presents Jesus issuing a call. He calls each and every one to share his life: "come with me," "labor with me." Life with Christ, labor with Christ, can be carried out in a variety of ways depending on the variety of calls, but it is understood very concretely of "preaching in synagogues, villages, and towns"; it moves "those who wish to give greater proof of their love and to distinguish themselves" to the desire of sharing Christ's redeeming life down to its ultimate consequences: "bearing all wrongs and all abuse and all poverty."[3]

The echo of Matthew 10, and the mission of the Apostles it describes, is heard even more clearly in the meditation on the Two Standards. It is a meditation for the discernment of spirits. It would have been enough to say that the evil spirit (or bad angel) leads a person to the desire of riches and honor and thence to overweening pride, and on the contrary the good spirit (or good angel) inspires desires of poverty and humiliations, leading ultimately to humility.[4]

But then there are "so many persons, apostles, disciples, etc." whom Jesus "chooses" and "sends throughout the whole world to spread his sacred doctrine among all men, no matter what their state or condition," "recommending to them to seek to help all, first by attracting them to the highest spiritual poverty . . . , secondly . . . to a desire for insults and contempt, for from these springs humility. . . . From these three stages let them lead men to all other virtues."[5] We might say, in the language of the Constitutions, that he sends them "in order to be good and faithful sowers in the Lord's field and to preach his divine word"[6] endeavoring "to help and dispose souls to gain their ultimate end from the hand of God our Creator and Lord."[7]

Nadal says that Ignatius "understood his goal, the aim he should pursue in his every undertaking." As a matter of fact, he immediately started to spread the teachings of the Gospel and to help souls. He went even further: he wanted to follow literally in the footsteps of Jesus and the Apostles, helping souls in the Holy Land, in the very villages and towns where the Lord had taught.[8] When he realized that that was not God's will,

2 Mt 9:35-10:9.
3 Cf. Sp Ex 95-98.
4 Cf. SpEx 313-327.
5 SpEx 145-146.
6 Exam ch. 2, n. 6 [30]; 5, n. 6 [109].
7 Const P. I, 2, n. 8 [156]; cf. Exam 1, n. 3 [4]; Const P. X, 2 [813].
8 Cf. Autobiog 45.

he started to study "so that he would be able to help souls,"[9] convinced as he was that "to fulfill the function of sowing and dispensing the divine word and of attending to the spiritual aid of one's neighbors, it is expedient to possess a sufficiency of sound learning."[10] In the meantime, however, he did not cease teaching catechism and giving the Exercises, and when told he could not, he left Alcalá and Salamanca and moved on to Paris. Some of his retreatants were young students who felt that they too were called by Christ to share his life and go "throughout the whole world to spread his sacred doctrine" and help souls. This is how the first group of companions was gathered, bound by this same ideal.

But just then came the crisis. There was agreement as to the kind of life they ought to live; but where? Fr. Simão Rodrigues, whose record of the discussion has been preserved, says that some of them had a very strong desire to bring the light of the Gospel to unbelievers (which probably included Muslims as well).[11] Others were inclined to help the souls of the faithful or preferred not to limit the scope of their preaching. Finally they thought of the pope as offering a solution: they would report to the pope "so that His Holiness might send them wherever he thought God would be best served."[12]

This is the situation Ignatius had in mind ten years later, when he wrote: "Coming from diverse countries and provinces and knowing not which regions to go to or stay in, among the faithful or unbelievers, in order not to err in the way of the Lord, and because we were not sure where we could best serve and praise God our Lord through his divine grace, we made this promise or vow that His Holiness might distribute or send us for the greater glory of God our Lord, in accordance with our promise and intention to travel through the world, and if we did not find the desired spiritual fruit in one city or the other, to pass on to another and yet another, and so on and so forth, going about through cities and other particular places for the greater glory of God our Lord and the greater spiritual profit of souls."[13]

They were possibly under the impression that the pope would solve the difficulty by assigning a field of apostolate to the entire group, in a Christian or a non-Christian country. But Paul III began to send them individually, keeping these "missions" to himself. This fact precipitated

---

9 Ibid 50.
10 Exam ch. 5, n. 6 [109].
11 MI FontNarr III 20-23;
12 Polanco in FontNarr I 185; cf. Autobiog 85.
13 "Constitutiones circa missiones" 1 (MI Const I 160).

events; perhaps that was why Ignatius called it "our principle and main foundation."[14]

So far the companions had been held together by their common ideals and the bond of spiritual friendship. They were "friends in the Lord."[15] What would become of the group after the pope decided to send one here and another there? Would it dissolve, if each one was left to himself?

In the Lent of the year 1539 they decided to meet every evening (the day was taken up by spiritual ministries) in order to deliberate on this vital question. The solution came quickly and easily. On the very first evening they decided that they ought not undo the union God had made but rather strengthen it further, "making themselves into a body." But what kind of body? A religious institute? At this point the difficulties became much greater.   They feared that they would be forced to embrace one of the ancient Rules, and that would come in the way of their apostolic vocation. In fact the decree of the IV Lateran Council, confirmed by the II Council of Lyons, was still in force, namely, that whoever wanted to found a new religious order would have to adopt one of the Rules already approved.[16] Finally, after many lengthy discussions, they decided to add to the vows of poverty and chastity, which they already had, a vow of obedience to the one they would elect as superior of the group; by that action they would effectively become a religious order.[17] In this way the vocation they had received in the Exercises and had so far followed without any juridical bonds would now become institutionalized in a juridical body, a religious order.

This is the point at which the Formula of the Institute came into existence.

1. The First Draft (F39)

The next step after that momentous decision was to determine the basic outline of the Institute and submit it to the Holy See for approval. And so they continued meeting every evening until June 24, the feast of St. John the Baptist.[18] Pierre Favre, who may have chaired the meetings, made a brief summary of the resolutions taken in two conclusive sessions,

---

14 Ibid 162.
15 Expression used by Ignatius before the foundation of the Society as a religious order in a letter to Juan Verdolay dated July 1537 (MI Epp I 119).
16 IV Lateran Council (1215), const. 13; II Council of Lyons (1274), const. 23.
17 Cf. "Deliberatio primorum patrum": MI Const I 1-8.
18 Cf. ibid 7, n. 9.

May 3 and June 11.[19] There must have been one more on June 24, but we do not know the outcome because Pierre Favre, together with Laínez, left Rome four days earlier on a papal mission, and no one replaced him.

It was at those meetings, held between April 15 and June 24, 1539, or immediately afterwards, that the first Fathers made the first draft of the Formula,[20] "according to what experience had shown them to be more expedient for the aim they had set themselves."[21] That was how they put it and so it came about: the Formula states the aim they had proposed to themselves, or rather the aim the Lord had proposed to them in the Exercises and the points they decided on later as how better to achieve that end.

They divided the Formula into five "chapters" or articles and a conclusion.

The first chapter presents the aim, the apostolic vocation. But since it had been resolved to institutionalize this vocation, living it in a body, a religious order, the second part sets forth the essential features of this institutionalization: a superior, a set of rules, the superior's council.

Chapter 2 deals with the vow of obedience to the pope. That was their first decision in the meeting of May 3.[22]

The topic of chapter 3 is the vow of obedience to the superior, but there is a long paragraph recommending the teaching of catechism. No reference to the former is be found in the sessions of May 9 and June 4, possibly because it had already been discussed in the deliberations held during Lent. But several rather concrete decisions were taken regarding the teaching of catechism at the session of May 3.[23]

On June 11 they decided what the Society's poverty should be like.[24] This point is covered in chapter 4 of the Formula.

The rest of the Formula must have been discussed at the meeting on June 24, of which we have no information. The topics are the following: exception in favor of scholastics as regards poverty (second part of chapter 4); exclusion of choir and solemn church services (chapter 5); recommendation not to impose austerities and not to admit to profession except after many probations (conclusion).

---

19 MI Const I 9-14. He also recorded the resolution taken on May 23, though of a rather procedural character.
20 This first draft has been published in MI Const I 16-20.
21 In the draft of the apostolic letters in which they included the Formula : MI Const I 16, lines 31-32.
22 MI Const I 10-11.
23 Ibid 11-12.
24 Ibid 13.

Because of the division into chapters, this first Formula came to be known as "The Five Chapters."

When drafted it was submitted for examination to the Dominican Tommaso Badía, Master of the Sacred Palace, who certified that "the Society's intent was pious and holy."[25]

Pope Paul III granted his approval at Tivoli, where he happened to be at the time in the company of Cardinal Gaspar Contarini. Ignatius sent both the Formula and Badía's opinion to the cardinal. Contarini replied on September 3, 1539: "I had a meeting with His Holiness today and, besides making an oral request, I read him all the Five Chapters. His Holiness liked them very much and very kindly approved and confirmed them."[26] According to other sources, Paul III is said to have added: "The Spirit of God is here"[27] and he expressed the hope that the new congregation would bring about reform of the Church.[28]

This oral approval has, beyond its theological value, more juridical importance than some might imagine. An oral approval attested in writing by a cardinal has full validity in law.[29] So Ignatius had every reason to write to his nephew Beltrán a few days later: "The vicar of Christ our Lord has approved and confirmed our whole manner of proceeding. . . . He has granted full faculties for drawing up constitutions which according to our judgment will be adapted to our way of life."[30]

2. The Second Draft (F40)

Nonetheless, the obstacles that rose when it came to obtaining written approval seemed insurmountable.

Cardinal Girolamo Ghinucci, the one who had to draw up the bull or brief, took objection to three items: the special vow of obedience to the pope and the exclusion both of solemnity in worship and of austerities imposed by rule. He thought the first pointless since every Christian is obliged to obey the pope, and the other two, he feared, could be interpreted as confirming Protestant errors.[31] There must have been other

---

25 MI Const I 16, lines 39-43.
26 Ibid 21-22. The cardinal wrote much the same words at the end of the document containing the Formula. Ibid 21.
27 Nadal in 1554: MHSI Nadal V 49.
28 Polanco in 1547: MI FontNarr I 206.
29 Cf. CIC (1917) c. 79 (c. 74 in the 1983 Code), coll. can. 239, n. 17.
30 MI Epp I 149. Salmerón used similar language when writing to Laínez: ibid 154. (English translation: *Letters of St. Ignatius of Loyola*, Selected and Translated by William J. Young, S.J., Loyola University Press, Chicago, 1959; p. 40.)
31 Cf. F. Dittrich, *Regesten und Briefe des Cardinals Contarini* (Braunsberg 1881) 304-305.

objections and other objectors besides Ghinucci. The pope named Cardinal Bartolomeo Guidiccioni to solve the impasse. But it was like running up to Scylla to avoid Charybdis. Guidiccioni was decidedly opposed to the multiplication of religious orders and based his opposition on the conciliar decrees we have mentioned.

Ignatius resorted to prayer and promised to celebrate no less than 3,000 Masses. At the same time he applied all human means of persuasion and secured testimonials from princes and cities where Jesuits had been working.

Finally Cardinal Guidiccioni relented. He even spoke to the pope in favor of the Society early in September 1540, together with Cardinals Contarini and Pio di Carpi. The bull of approval *Regimini Militantis Ecclesiae* was issued on September 27 and contained the full text of the Formula, although with a few changes or corrections.[32]

It is on account of these changes or corrections—not because it is a new formulation of the matter, as the word might imply—that we have called it "second draft." We shall duly point out the changes as we go along. Suffice it to state for the moment that they can be divided into three categories.

First, there are the changes due to Cardinal Ghinucci's scruples. A more explicit justification of the vow of obedience to the pope is added, and the two paragraphs regarding solemn worship and common exterior life are omitted.

Other changes may have been required by the "stylus curiae" and show a desire for greater accuracy. For instance, "Roman pontiff" is added to "vicar of Christ"; public preaching and confessions are mentioned explicitly when listing apostolic ministries; when speaking of the vow of special obedience to the pope this clarification is added: "to whatsoever provinces they may choose to send us"; it is explicitly stated that everything is subject to the good pleasure of the Apostolic See.

Finally, there is a change that implies an evolution in the Institute. The colleges have come into existence, and they, not the Society, will own the income for the support of scholastics.

3. The Third Draft (F50)

Ignatius and his companions foresaw in 1541 that the Formula would have to be revised in the light of experience and the evolution of the

---

32 Critical edition of the bull in MI Const I 24-32.

Institute.[33] This revision could not be effected until 1547, when Ignatius was given efficient help in the person of Juan Alfonso Polanco.

Polanco started work with his characteristic zest. He wrote out each point of F40 and below each, in shorter lines, the remarks and questions connected with them. He showed his work to Ignatius and took down his answers. This is what the editor of *Monumenta Historica* has termed Polanco's third series of doubts or questions.[34] Polanco was not satisfied with this. He had the same questions and remarks copied out along with the answers given orally by Ignatius, and he submitted them to the latter for further consideration. Then Ignatius wrote down the final solution in his own hand, correcting, completing, or confirming the solution previously given. This is called the fourth series of doubts.[35]

Sometimes Ignatius chose to consult canon lawyers. The answers two of them gave were collected in the sixth series.[36]

These documents enable us to see the reason for almost every single change made in the Formula.

Ignatius lets us see the spirit in which they were working in a letter of July 1549 to Francis Borgia. He tells him that "even in the bulls [that is, in the Formula] some points are being revised" and he goes on to describe the method he used in these words: "recommending the whole matter to God our Lord with many Masses, prayers, and tears; what is aimed at is not a relaxing of what has been well founded, but a greater perfection, so that we may go from good to better for God's greater glory." (These words were written in his own hand.)[37]

In this way about a hundred changes were made; we shall note them in due course. They can be divided into four categories. Some are due to the desire to have a fuller and more accurate exposition of various aspects of the Institute, such as its aim and means, the powers of the general congregation and the superior general, the purpose of the colleges, the priestly character of the Society. . . . Others take note of developments that had taken place since 1540, regarding three points mainly: poverty, the admission of coadjutors, and the appointment of subordinate superiors. The third group consists of permissions sought: to interpret the Formula,

---

33 Cf. MI Const I 45-46.

34 MI Const I 295-317. I shall refer to them as Dubiorum Series Tertia. The first two series comprised other suggestions about the Institute; those of the second were based on the rules and constitutions of other religious orders.

35 MI Const I 319-339.

36 Ibid 346-355. The fifth series consists of a consultation with Fr. Egidio Foscarari, O.P., about the account of conscience.

37 MI Epp XII 645 (Young, p. 206).

to open colleges where there is no university, and to consider these colleges as established through the authorization of the Holy See. Finally, some changes were made to avoid disedification, e.g., explaining the reason why the vow of obedience to the pope is made. This revised Formula was approved by Julius III on July 21, 1550, through the bull "Exposcit Debitum," which included it in full.[38] In this bull the pope states once again that the new Formula expresses the Society's institute more accurately and clearly "because of the lessons learned through experience and usage, but in the same spirit."[39]

II. SIGNIFICANCE OF THE FORMULA

The Formula of the Institute is the Rule of the Society: that is to say, it corresponds to what the legislation of the old religious orders called the Rule. Some historians have denied this.[40] But the Society has officially endorsed this view in three General Congregations: V (1593-1594), XXVII (1923), and XXXI (1965-1966).[41]

Ignatius himself and his companions call it by this name: "this Rule of ours." This is what Francis Xavier called it when, writing from India, he said he was happy to learn that "our Rule" had been confirmed.[42] This is also what Pope Pius VII called it in the bull of restoration of the Society, "Sollicitudo omnium ecclesiarum."

Apart from the name, this is what Ignatius and his companions give us to understand when, right at the end of the Formula, they state what they had in mind when writing it. They say, in fact, that they want to present "a kind of sketch" of our profession, that is, the principal features of the Institute of the Society. GC 31 was right to state that "the Formula exhibits the fundamental structure of the Society, based, with the help of grace, on Gospel principles and the experience and wisdom of our holy Father Ignatius and his companions."[43] What else is a Rule?

Our first Fathers may on the whole have avoided calling it the Rule because, according to the conciliar decrees officially in force, any new foundation was supposed to adopt an existing Rule. They preferred to call

---

38 Critical edition in MI Const I 373-383.
39 Ibid 375. I have developed the ideas of this first part of the Introduction in my article "Origine e storia della Formula dell'Istituto" in *La Formula dell'Istituto*, CIS, Rome 1977 9-31.
40 Cf. P. Tacchi Venturi, *Storia della Compagnia di Gesù in Italia* II/I (Rome 1950) 295.
41 GC V, d. 58; GC XXVII, Coll. Decr., d. 12; GC XXXI, d. 4, n. 2.
42 MHSI EppXav I 87; cf. 176.
43 GC XXXI, d. 4, n. 3.

it Formula or way of life (*formula vivendi, forma vitae*).[44] At the beginning this expression was meant to indicate the way of life contained in the document; later on it designated the document that contained it, whereas the way of life was called "Institute" (*institutum vitae*). This explains the phrase introduced in the final draft of the Formula: "Our Institute as comprised in this Formula." This is how the expression "Formula of the Institute" was coined and later consecrated by usage. It is interesting to note that the expressions "formula or way of life" are to be found in the papal approval of St. Clare's Rule.[45]

Confirming a decree of GC 5, GC 27 declared that "the substantials of our Institute are, first of all, the matters contained in the Formula or Rule of the Society submitted to Julius III and approved by him and many of his successors, and also that without which the matters contained in the Formula cannot be maintained or not without difficulty."

What did GC 27 mean by "substantials"? Did it use the word in the philosophical or in the juridical sense?

Substantial, in the philosophical sense, is whatever constitutes the substance of something, that without which it would cease to be what it is. Juridically, substance is what belongs to the fundamental law of a group; the law cannot be altered if the group is to preserve its identity. The acts of the commission that prepared the decree state in so many words that the congregation meant to use juridical, not philosophical, language. This is why it also used the word "institutional." Substantial to the Institute is, therefore, whatever belongs to the Formula of the Institute, which is its Rule and fundamental law, and in the second place whatever is intimately related to it either as a necessary or a very conducive condition.

What is the relationship between the Formula of the Institute and the Constitutions? In the Society, as we have just explained, the Formula corresponds to what other orders have called the Rule. But their model as it stands cannot be applied to the Society. In the old orders the Rule and the Constitutions are vastly differing documents not only as regards their length but also as regards their purpose and author, and hence their juridical and spiritual importance. To speak only of the three major orders that had the greatest influence on the Society's Institute, the Rule of the Benedictines is the work of the great patriarch of western monasticism St. Benedict, whereas the various constitutions came much later (under this or that name of statutes, customs . . .) to regulate the life of the various monasteries or monastic congregations that came into existence. In the

44 Cf. MI Const I 16, 20, 67.
45 Cf. *Seraphicae legislationis textus originales* (Ad Aquas Claras, 1899) 49-50.

Order of Preachers the Rule is that of St. Augustine; the Constitutions were composed by St. Dominic and the general chapters in order to determine what is specific to the Dominican vocation. As for the Franciscans, the Rule was written by the founder, St. Francis; the Constitutions came 34 years after his death and are the work of St. Bonaventure, who had them approved by the general chapter at Narbonne in 1260.

In the Society the founder is the author both of the Formula and of the Constitutions; the Formula refers to the Constitutions again and again: "as will be explained in the Constitutions," "as will be explained more fully in the Constitutions." As a result, in the Constitutions the founder gives us the exact interpretation of what might be doubtful in the Formula, as he understands it himself.[46] He specifies what is said more generally in the Formula;[47] he explains and completes what the Formula may have left implicit. In that sense the Constitutions suppose the Formula. The opening paragraph of Part VI of the Constitutions in the primitive text is interesting in this connection. It stated as follows: "Though the bull of our Institute [the Formula] contains the substance of what must be observed in the Lord in this Society, some points of the said bull will be declared more fully here."[48] The Constitutions can be said to be the Formula expounded and developed by the author himself.

46 Cf. for instance Const P. IV, 2, F [330]; P. V, 3, C [529].
47 Cf. for instance Const P. VIII, 3, n. 1 [682].
48 MI Const II 202.

THE FIRST CHAPTER:
THE AIM OF THE SOCIETY AND
ITS INSTITUTIONALIZATION

This chapter is clearly divided into two parts: the aim of the Society and its institutionalization.

I. THE AIM OF THE SOCIETY

This first part describes the aim of the Society, its vocation: all that, according to Nadal's words in 1554, God taught its founder during the Exercises at Manresa, and specifically in the meditations on the Kingdom and on the Two Standards. Ignatius pursued this aim and observed this way of life from then on; so did the companions he recruited, even before the Society was formally founded, from their Paris and Venice days.

Note: Structure of the Text

The Formula is not written in an abstract sort of way, as for example: "the aim of the Society is. . . ." Like St. Benedict's Rule, it is addressed to those who wish to join the Society. The whole of this first part of chapter 1 is contained in a single sentence with a single subject: "Whoever desires . . ." and three main verbs: "should keep in mind," "should show himself ready," and "let any such person take care." The object of the first verb is a listing of the specific aims and means of the Society; that of the second, its activities; that of the third, the earnestness with which this aim is to be pursued.

1. The Subject

The subject is the person who wishes to become a member of the Society:

"Whoever desires to serve as a soldier of God beneath the banner of the cross in our Society—which we desire to be designated by the name of Jesus—and to serve the Lord

alone and the Church, His spouse, under the Roman pontiff,
the vicar of Christ on earth . . ."

"To serve as a soldier of God" (*militare Deo*) is a medieval expression meaning religious life. In the prologue of his Rule, St. Benedict addresses the novice who is "about to join battle for Christ the true King."[1] In the 13th century the Dominican Etienne de Salagnac spoke of "the many and various Rules under which religious wage war for God in the Church," and of the Rule of St. Augustine according to which "various cathedral and religious churches [i.e., canons and monks] battle for God."[2] The expression (*militare Deo*) is taken from St. Paul's "nemo militans Deo implicat se negotiis saecularibus."[3]

The words "under the banner of the Cross" echo those of the liturgical hymn "Vexilla Regis prodeunt," but we also detect an echo of the meditation on the Two Standards: "to be received under His standard."[4]

"Our Society, which we desire to be designated by the name of Jesus." According to Polanco, when our Fathers were at Vicenza in 1537, "it seemed to them that, since they had no head among themselves nor any other superior but Jesus Christ, whom alone they desired to serve, they should take the name of the One they had as their head and call themselves 'the Company of Jesus.'"[5] Laínez, however, links the name to the vision at La Storta, a few months later, when Ignatius was approaching Rome. After describing that spiritual experience, he adds: "Because of this, having great devotion to this most holy name, he wanted the group to be called the Company of Jesus."[6] It may be that at La Storta Ignatius understood better the profound meaning of the name they had chosen earlier.

The word "company" was common at the time in Italy to designate a pious association. The "Company of Divine Love" was well known. At first the order of the Theatines was known by the name of company and at Vicenza alone there were at least eight associations, all called companies, one of which was called "Company of the Name of Jesus and St. Joseph."

Ignatius was using this word in the same generic sense when he spoke of the "companies" of St. Francis and St. Dominic. He also called the various associations he founded in Rome "companies"; the "Company of

---

1 St. Benedict, *Regula*, prol., 3.
2 *MonOPHist* 22, 171-172.
3 2 Tim 2:4. The best Greek manuscripts do not have the word "God."
4 SpEx 147.
5 MI Font Narr I 204.
6 C. de Dalmases, "Le esortazioni del P. Laínez sull'Examen Constitutionum" in AHSI 35 (1966) 137-138.

Grace," for instance. The word was therefore correctly translated in Latin as "Societas." The military connotation, of a company of soldiers, came later on and it contributed significantly to the misrepresentation of both the Institute and its founder. What is really important, of course, is the name of Jesus. It would not matter calling it the association, the congregation, or the order of Jesus. It is a group that has taken the name of Jesus as its distinguishing and identifying mark, and this is what the Latin original of the Formula means when it says: "Jesu nomine insigniri." Hence, even though the documents do speak of the "companions of Jesus," this expression is admissible only inasmuch as a servant can be called his master's companion, or a soldier his captain's. This was the answer sent from Rome to the Faculty of Theology at Paris in January 1556: "it is not called the Company of Jesus because we have made ourselves Jesus' companions but inasmuch as a squadron is called after its chief, whom we mean to follow by our Institute."[7]

Polanco, when reflecting on the importance Ignatius attached to this name, wrote: "Regarding this matter of the name, our Father Ignatius received so many visitations from the One whose name they took and so many signs of approval and confirmation of this name that I heard him say that he felt he would be going against God's will and offending him if he were to doubt of the fitness of this name. And when people told him and wrote to him that it should be changed because some said we took Jesus for ourselves and others made other accusations, I remember him saying that, if all the members of the Society (or anyone else we are not obliged under pain of sin to follow) judged that this name ought to be changed, he alone would never yield on this, and that since it is in the Constitutions that nothing may be done if one person objects,[8] this name would not be changed during his lifetime." Polanco adds: "As a rule, Father Master Ignatius has this firm assurance in matters he knows through means superior to human ones."[9]

The name "Society of Jesus" was explicitly approved by Gregory XIV in the bull "Ecclesiae Catholicae."

The next phrase "and to serve the Lord alone . . ." contains the first change in the Formula. F39 and F40 read: "to serve the Lord alone and the Roman pontiff, his vicar on earth." Polanco suggested that this could be taken as smacking of flattery; others too, besides the pope, made use of the Society, the bishops for instance. Ignatius replied that the phrase could

---

7   MI Epp XII 615.
8   He was thinking of the 1541 Constitutions, n. 45: MI Const I 47.
9   MI FontNarr I 204.

be reworded "to convey the meaning that we ought to serve the whole Church but as being under the supreme vicar of Christ."[10]

This, then, is the origin of the change made in F50. But it is not as great as might seem at first sight. It makes explicit what was only implicit in the previous text. The Society serves the Church inasmuch as it is the Spouse of Christ, one thing with Him, and inasmuch as it is under Christ's vicar, who is the universal shepherd, to whom Christ has entrusted the whole of His flock. By serving the Church, the Society serves Christ and his vicar on earth. It is therefore a moot point whether the words "under the Roman pontiff" should be referred to the verb "to serve," as is usually done, or rather to "the Church," that is, the Church as being under the Roman pontiff.

It may be argued that the Society also helps heretics and unbelievers outside the Church. But at that time the Church was not thought of as an institution placed in the midst of the world to help mankind. Men either belonged to the Church (the Catholics) or were destined to be its members (heretics and infidels). By helping the latter one worked for their membership in the Church and thus served the Church.

2. The Aims and Specific Means

Whoever desires to be a member of the Society

> "should, after a solemn vow of perpetual chastity, poverty, and obedience, keep what follows in mind. He is a member of a Society founded chiefly for this purpose: to strive especially for the defense and propagation of the faith and for the progress of souls in Christian life and doctrine, by means of public preaching, lectures, and any other ministration whatsoever of the word of God, and further by means of the Spiritual Exercises, the education of children and unlettered persons in Christianity, and the spiritual consolation of Christ's faithful through hearing confessions and administering the other sacraments."

The prospective candidate should understand what are the aims and means proper to the Society, a member of which he becomes "after a solemn vow of perpetual chastity, poverty, and obedience."

"A solemn vow." When F39 and F40 were drafted, only the professed were considered to be members of the Society. The coadjutors came later on, in 1546, and the scholastics were regarded as young aspirants. This has

---

10 *Dubiorum Series Tertia:* MI Const I 299-300; *Series Quarta,* n. 15: ibid 322.

to be kept in mind throughout the Formula. A paragraph about the coadjutors was added at the end of the final draft (F50), as we shall see.

"Of perpetual chastity, poverty, and obedience." F39 and F40 spoke only of "perpetual chastity," either because the other two vows were discussed further on (in chapters 3 and 4) or rather because that of chastity realizes and best shows one's personal attachment to Christ, one's definitive commitment to Him. It is also the first that is usually made when someone wants to consecrate himself to God and the first vow Ignatius made, shortly after his conversion, on the way from Loyola to Montserrat.[11] However, once the Society had been founded as a religious order, the three vows were taken together in the act of profession.[12] This is why, when F50 was being prepared and Polanco asked Ignatius about it, Ignatius wished the matter to be referred to canonist Giacomo del Pozzo for consultation, though he was inclined to put them together in the Formula, and so it was in fact done.[13]

a. The Aim

The Society which one joins by making the solemn vows of chastity, poverty, and obedience was "founded chiefly for this purpose: to strive especially for the defense and propagation of the faith and for the progress of souls in Christian life and doctrine."

The word "defense" was added in F50. F39 and F40 did not have it, even though our first Fathers had defended the faith in Rome back in 1538 against Agostino Mainardi's teachings.[14] The order in which the aims are stated has also been changed. It may have been considered more logical to speak first of faith, which is the foundation, and then of deepening it and living up to it. Did the original doublet—the progress of souls and the propagation of the faith—reflect the two tendencies that came to the fore among the group of companions, and were the object of so many discussions in Paris?:[15] they "did not know into which regions they were to go, whether among the faithful or the unbelievers."[16]

This is the double or triple aim the Constitutions mean when they speak of "giving aid toward the salvation and perfection of the souls of

---

11 Laínez in MI FontNarr I 75.
12 Const P. V, ch. 3, n. 3 [527].
13 *Dubiorum Series Tertia*, n. 1: MI Const I 302; *Series Quarta*, n. 24: ibid 324.
14 Cf. Tacchi Venturi, *Storia della Compagnia di Gesù in Italia*, II/I, Rome 1950, 139-144.
15 Cf. Simão Rodrigues in MI FontNarr III 20-23.
16 Const P. VII, ch. 1, B [605].

their fellowmen,"[17] "helping and disposing souls to gain their ultimate end from the hand of God our Creator and Lord,"[18] "aiding souls to reach their ultimate and supernatural end."[19] It is not human development in the natural order that is meant, but our fellowmen's right ordering in God.

b. Specific Means

F39 read: "by means of the ministry of the word, the Spiritual Exercises, and works of charity and specifically *(nominatim)* by means of the education of children and unlettered persons in Christianity."

F40 added "public preaching" and "the spiritual consolation of Christ's faithful through hearing confessions." In fact, even before 1539 the first Fathers used to administer the sacrament of penance.[20]

F50 drew a clearer distinction between the spiritual ministries and the works of charity: it linked this latter paragraph to the previous ones and transferred the listing of the works of charity, in a more developed form, to the following paragraph. It also added "lectures" to preaching, and the administration of other sacraments to that of hearing confessions. But it dropped the word "nominatim" (specifically) when referring to the teaching of Christian doctrine. We shall see why.

Practically speaking, everything is reduced to the ministry of the word and the administration of the sacraments, and as regards the latter to its prophetic, rather than to its cultic, aspect. As to the ministry of the word, preaching and lectures are mentioned by name, but adding in a general way: "and any other ministration of the word of God." The Spiritual Exercises are mentioned separately, presumably on account of the personalized way in which they were given. (The Constitutions put them along with spiritual conversations.)[21] The teaching of catechism is also mentioned apart, probably because of the importance attributed to this ministry in F39 and F40.

"Ministration of the word of God" is a biblical expression. The Acts of the Apostles relate how in the dispute over the assistance given to the widows the Apostles said: "It would not be right for us to neglect the word of God so as to give out food. . . . We will continue to devote ourselves to prayer and to the service of the word."[22]

17 Exam ch. 1, n. 2 [3].
18 Const P. I, ch. 2, n. 8 [156].
19 Const P. X, n. 2 [813].
20 Cf. MI Const I 16, lines 15-16.
21 Cf. Const P. VII, ch. 4, n. 8 [648].
22 Cf. Acts 6:2; cf. ibid 20:24 (Vulg.)

F40 added "of God" to "ministration of the word," whereby the expression loses some of its New Testament resonance.

"Lectures" means "sacred lectures" on a book from Holy Scripture since it is immediately followed by "and any other ministration of the word of God." Classroom lectures are not "ministrations of the word of God." This is confirmed by a parallel contemporary text mentioning "sacred lectures" among these ministries.[23]

Nadal explains the difference between lectures and sacred lectures, and between public preaching and sacred lectures.[24]

As we have already remarked and shall see better in chapter 3, F39 and F40 emphasized the teaching of Christian doctrine by adding "specifically" (*nominatim*), which adverb was dropped in F50. This added emphasis might have been due partly to the reasons we shall review in chapter 3 and partly also to the fact that the pope had asked the first Fathers to undertake the catechizing of the children of Rome.[25]

The way the sacrament of penance is referred to is remarkable: "the spiritual consolation of Christ's faithful through hearing confessions." Ignatius defines spiritual consolation as an encouragement to act well, to serve God better.[26] The ministry of hearing confessions goes beyond merely forgiving sins to exhorting and helping a person to advance in Christian living. This fits in perfectly with the "ministry of the word."

The reference to "the other sacraments" seems to have been added in F50 in order to put together all the faculties previously granted by the popes.[27] If we except the sacrament of penance and that of the Eucharist (normally administered within the Mass), all the other sacraments belong either to the parish or to a bishop and are, therefore, less proper to the Society. In fact the Constitutions mention only confession and Communion.[28]

These aims and means can be expressed in one single word: evangelization. They coincide with those indicated by Paul VI in the Apostolic Exhortation *Evangelii Nuntiandi*. For that reason Ignatius states in the Constitutions that one enters the Society "in order to be a good and faithful sower in the Lord's field and to preach His divine word."[29]

---

23 MI Const I 183, lines 8-9.
24 Cf. MHSI Nadal V 380-382.
25 Polanco in MI FontNarr I 197.
26 Cf. SpEx 315.
27 Cf. MI Const I 375, lines 71-72.
28 Cf. Const P. IV, ch. 8, n. 4 [406]; P. VII, ch. 4, n. 5 [642].
29 Exam ch. 2, n. 6 [30]; cf. ch. 5, n. 6 [109].

c. The Three Adverbs

In the preceding explanation we have passed over two adverbs: chiefly (*potissimum*) and especially (*praecipue*). And there is still a third: moreover (*nihilominus*). These adverbs are important for an understanding of the structure of the paragraph.

There seems to be some redundancy in the use of the first two: "founded chiefly . . . to strive especially." Some try to avoid the redundancy by referring the first adverb to the aims and the second one to the means: "founded chiefly for the defense . . . , especially by means of public preaching. . . ." The original Latin does admit this interpretation but it is somewhat forced and I do not think it is necessary. All the ministries are presented as means since they are introduced by the preposition "per" (by means of). Polanco so names them.[30] Nadal, on the contrary, considers these ministries as immediate aims serving more longterm ones;[31] as though one said: the Society has been founded to perform the ministry of the word and thereby defend and propagate the faith and further the progress of souls in Christian life and doctrine. All this constitutes one single aim: evangelization. Reference is made to this further below no less than three times and always in the singular: "this aim." The two adverbs are there to emphasize that this is the specific aim of the Society and that everything must be geared to it.

The third adverb ("nihilominus") can be translated either as "nonetheless" or "moreover." In any case it is meant to set the second sentence (he should show himself ready) against the first (should keep in mind), contrasting the tasks listed in the second sentence with those listed in the first. Nadal stresses it forcefully when he writes: "*Potissmum* [chiefly] refers to *nihilominus* [moreover] further below and is meant to point out that the Society undertakes those special activities with primary intensity, in the first place, more earnestly than the others, which must be given second place and undertaken when the former allow, if we cannot do justice to both."[32]

3. Secondary Activities

"Moreover, he should show himself ready to reconcile the estranged, compassionately assist and serve those in prisons or hospitals, and indeed to perform any other works of

---

30   *Dubiorum Series Tertia:* MI Const I 296, lines 22-31.

31   MHSI Nadal V 341.

32   Cf. Manuel Ruiz Jurado, *Nadal y Polanco sobre la Fórmula del Instituto de la Compañía de Jesús,* in AHSI 47 (1978) 237; cf. MHSI Nadal V 862.

charity, according to what will seem expedient for the glory
of God and the common good."

This paragraph was added in F50. F39 and F40 referred only vaguely
to the works of charity, along with the spiritual ministries of the preceding
paragraph. When the draft for F50 was being prepared, Polanco inquired
from Ignatius whether it might be good to mention other means explicitly,
such as visiting prisons and hospitals and reconciling the estranged,
frequent activities among the Jesuits in Rome. Ignatius hesitated at first;
then he replied in the affirmative, but he cautioned: "no obligation should
be implied."[33] This directive was complied with not only through the use
of the adverbs we have just examined but also through the very formulation of the sentence. The previous sentence declared that the Jesuit must
keep in mind that the Society to which he belongs has been founded to
achieve certain specific spiritual aims through certain specific means (for
evangelization). Now he is merely told that he must "show himself ready"
to take up these other activities as well, and that just "according to what
will seem expedient for the glory of God and the common good." The
Constitutions give the same secondary and subordinate rank to these
activities.[34]

4. Gratuity

"Furthermore, all these works should be carried out
altogether free of charge and without accepting any remuneration for the labor expended in all the aforementioned
activities."

"All these works" could be interpreted as referring to the works of
charity only, but "all the aforementioned activities" excludes all doubt:
spiritual ministries are also included. Besides, their gratuity is very clearly
stated in the Constitutions.[35]

The early Society was seized by the idea that our Institute aimed at
imitating the life-style and activities of the Apostles. As noted in the
Introduction, Ignatius seems to have been inspired by Matthew 10, where
the Lord in sending the Apostles to preach the Gospel instructs them to
cast out devils and cure the sick, but warns them to give out freely what
they have freely received. The Society's aim is to evangelize. Its members,
as we shall see in chapter 2, are sent by the vicar of Christ just as the

33 *Dubiorum Series Tertia:* MI Const I 297; *Series Quarta*, n. 2: ibid 319.
34 Const P. VII, ch. 4, n. 9 [650].
35 Const P. VI, ch. 2, n. 7 [565].

Apostles were sent by Christ himself. The Society is also engaged in comforting the sick in body and soul (as F39 put it). And it does all of this gratuitously, as it has gratuitously received it. The Constitutions use the very words of the Gospel.[36] In fact, Ignatius would have liked to use them here, too, in the Formula.[37] The members of the Society do have power even to cast out devils and exercise it in the ministry of penance.[38] Rightly has it been said, then, that the aim (or charism) of the Society is to preach the Gospel in imitation of the Apostles.

5. Exhortation

> "Still further, let any such person take care, as long as he
> lives, first of all to keep before his eyes God and then the
> nature of this Institute which is . . . a pathway to God; and
> then let him strive with all his effort to achieve this end set
> before him by God—each one, however, according to the
> grace which the Holy Spirit has given to him and according
> to the particular grade of his own vocation."

This third paragraph is introduced by the verb "curetque"—"let any such person take care"—and contains one or rather two points: one is a reflection for consideration by the mind; the other, a recommendation for execution by the will.

a. Reflection

"Whoever desires to serve as a soldier of God in our Society" must— keeping in mind what has so far been said about its aim—"take care, as long as he lives, first of all to keep before his eyes God and then the nature of this Institute which is a pathway to God."

"To keep before his eyes" is to gaze at the goal towards which one is running, the reference point of one's life and activity.

"As long as he lives." F39 and F40 read "always." It was changed so that it might not be interpreted as meaning "continuously," without interruption. It should guide us throughout our lives, in all our decisions, though we may not think about it uninterruptedly, all the time.[39]

"First of all . . . God." The Society does aim at helping men, but it should not rest there as in its ultimate goal, which is God alone; all the

---

36 Ibid.
37 MI Const I 272, line 75.
38 The thought is S. Lyonnet's, *Apóstoles de Jesucristo* 26.
39 *Dubiorum Series Tertia:* MI Const I 300; *Series Quarta*, n. 16: ibid 322.

Society's life and work ought to be oriented toward God. The Constitutions repeat these and similar expressions almost 300 times: glory, praise, honor, service of God.

"The nature of this Institute" is to be kept before the eyes, inasmuch as it is a pathway that leads to God: it leads the one who lives it to God, by his leading others to God. The Constitutions want the novice to be asked whether he wishes to enter the Society "for greater praise and glory of God our Lord and also that he may better serve and perfect his own soul by helping other souls, his neighbors."[40]

b. Recommendation

Having thus set the direction of his life, the Jesuit must "strive with all his effort to achieve this end set before him by God." What we have earlier called "aims and means" is termed "end," in the singular. It is God who sets this end before the Jesuit because it is God who calls him to this manner of life. The Jesuit must summon up all his energy in the defense and propagation of the faith and the progress of souls in Christian life and doctrine, through the ministry of God's word and the administration of the sacraments. In other words, he must spend all his energy in the work of evangelization.

"Each one, however, according to the grace which the Holy Spirit has given to him and according to the particular grade of his own vocation." "Each one of us has been given his own share of grace, given as Christ allotted it."[41] Each one has his own charism. Though the aim of the Institute is one and the same for everyone, God's call to pursue it with all one's energy allows for various shadings and nuances. Here in embryo is the distinction of grades, formally established in 1546 and referred to at the end of F50. I do not mean the word "grade" itself so much as the idea, here implicit, that the general vocation to evangelize allows for personal vocations as so many diverse ways of achieving it.

II. INSTITUTIONALIZATION

Our first Fathers began to realize the aim described in the first part of this chapter from the time that the Lord set it before them in the Exercises: Ignatius, since Manresa; the companions, since Paris.

---

40 Exam ch. 3, n. 15 [52].
41 Eph 4:7.

But, as I explained in the Introduction, because Paul III reserved the "missions" to himself and began to send them individually, the companions decided not to break up the group and sever their union but to strengthen it by constituting a "body"—a body that after many discussions was to take the form of a religious order. This was tantamount to institutionalizing this apostolic aim, this life ideal, by which they had so far lived without any juridical bonds.

The second part of the chapter shows the result of this decision. The institutionalization of the aim described in the first part requires three juridical institutions which are now described: a superior, a legislation, and a council or body that is deliberative or consultative. This explains why the Formula speaks twice of the superior: here considering his office in connection with authority, which is the form of every society, and in chapter 3 in its connection with the vow of obedience.

1. The Superior

> "Consequently, lest anyone should perhaps show zeal, but a zeal which is not according to knowledge, the decision about each one's grade and the selection and entire distribution of employments shall be in the power of the superior general or ordinary who at any future time is to be elected by us, or in the power of those whom this superior general may appoint under himself with that authority, in order that the proper order necessary in every well-organized community may be preserved."

Not only at this stage of its approval but also in the future the Society elects a "superior general or ordinary," and he and those he appoints "under himself with that authority" have power to decide "about each one's grade and the selection and entire distribution of employments."

When F39 and F40 were drafted, only one superior was envisaged. In 1546 Paul III granted permission for the appointment of subordinate superiors, both provincial and local. That is why F50 added the adjective "general" and the reference to those to whom the superior general can communicate his authority. It also added the words "at any time" because it was no longer the initial constitution of the group that was envisaged, but the future organization of the Society.

"Employments" here does not refer to house offices (those of minister, sacristan, doorkeeper, etc.), at least not exclusively, but to those of preacher, catechist, confessor. . . . A "determination" taken on 3 May 1539 and confirmed the next day read: "It must be left to the judgment of the superior of the Society whether, on arrival at a given place, one is to teach catechism, or preach, or perform some other ministry, or not."[42] Someone has interpreted this "determination" as indicating that the superior had, already at that stage, the power to send his men among the faithful.[43] But this faculty was not, in fact, applied for and obtained until 1542.[44] This proves rather that mission does not mean ministry but just "sending." The superior decides what ministry is to be performed by each one in his place of residence even if he might have been sent by the pope, unless of course the pope has already decided what ministry he ought to perform.

Polanco asked Ignatius if the superior's permission was always needed to exercise the ministries of the Society specified at the beginning of this chapter. The answer was that it was needed for habitually performing a ministry, such as preaching, but not for each individual act, for instance to preach a sermon or hear confessions on the occasions that might occur.[45]

Two reasons are adduced. The first is the possibility that someone might "perhaps show zeal, but a zeal which is not according to knowledge," a phrase taken from Romans 10:2 according to which the Jews have a misguided zeal (not according to knowledge), ignorant of the real relationship of men with God.

F39 and F40 placed this reason at the end of the previous paragraph, presenting it as the reason why each one must proceed according to the grace he has received and the grade of his vocation. After all, zeal without discretion is undiscerning love, in the language of the Constitutions.[46] By placing the phrase at the beginning of this paragraph and presenting it as the reason why the judgment on each one's grade should be left to the superior, F50 puts the burden on him rather than on the subject. That is why it is put as a consequence, following the need for each one to conform to the particular grade of his vocation: "consequently."

The second reason is "that the proper order necessary in every well-organized community may be preserved." The very word "order" is suggestive of the nature of the superior's authority and the corresponding obedience. This obedience has been called "corporative" to distinguish it from the "missional" obedience, discussed in chapter 2.[47] By the way,

---

42 MI Const I 11, n. 6.
43 F. Roustang, in S. Ignace de Loyola, *Constitutions de la Compagnie de Jésus* II (Coll. Christus, n. 24) 13.
44 Cf. MI FontDoc 657.
45 *Dubiorum Series Tertia:* MI Const I 297; *Series Quarta*, n. 4: ibid 319.
46 Cf. Const P. II, ch. 2, n. 5 [217].
47 Cf. J. Iturrioz, "Dos líneas de obediencia en la Compañía de Jesús," in *Manresa* 43 (1971) 59-78.

Ignatius never uses the word *community* in the restricted sense of a group of people living together in the same house, but in the more general sense of association or congregation.[48] F39 spoke of the whole Society as "community"; instead of saying "he is a member of a Society" it stated "he is a member of a community."

2. The Legislation

> "This superior general, with the council of his associates (with the majority of votes always having the right to prevail), shall possess the authority to establish constitutions leading to the achievement of this end which has been proposed to us. He shall also have the authority to explain officially doubts which may arise in connection with our Institute as comprised in this Formula."

It is taken for granted that there should be "constitutions leading to the achievement of this end which has been proposed to us." A misinterpretation of the preamble to the Constitutions[49] has led some into thinking that Ignatius, at first, did not want to write Constitutions: the interior law of charity should suffice.[50] These words of the Formula leave no room for doubt: the Constitutions are envisaged and desired right from the start. They were meant to ensure the achievement of the end that Ignatius and his companions set themselves. The Latin word translated as "achievement" is "constructio." The end (again in the singular, encompassing the aims and means set forth in the first part), that is, the kind of evangelical life referred to above, is viewed as the plan of a building that has to be constructed, an ideal that has to be put into practice. This requires Constitutions setting down specific norms, both spiritual and juridical—the master plan of the building. This end is described as having "been proposed to us"—in the passive form. The subject is not specified; perhaps it is God: this plan was proposed by God.

The superior general is given power to establish these Constitutions, but "with the council of his associates"; (F39 had said "his brethren"). The word "consilium" (or, in Spanish, "consejo") is used in this chapter with two different meanings: that of a deliberative and consultative body (council) and that of opinion or advice (counsel). In the passage that follows

---

48 Cf. Const P. IV, ch. 1, D [316]; P. VII, ch. 2, K [628]; P. IX, ch. 1, n. 1 [719]; P. X, n. 6 [817].

49 Const Preamble, n. 1 [134].

50 This opinion was refuted by A. Coemans, "Quandonam S. Ignatius decrevit leges scriptas dare," in AHSI I (1932) 304-306.

it is used with both meanings: the "council" has to be convoked to establish or change the Constitutions, the "counsel" of the brethren in matters of lesser importance. It might seem, at first sight, that this latter is the meaning it has in the present passage: counsel, advice;[51] but I am inclined to interpret it in the first meaning, of "council": the superior general with his associates gathered in council. That is why a majority of votes is said to be required for their decisions to have juridical validity. This norm is established for the writing of Constitutions; but the way it is put ("with the majority of votes always having the right to prevail") would seem to indicate that the directive is to be extended to other cases as well. F39 and F40 stated that the Constitutions had to be established "in consilio," i.e., convoking the council of the companions. This expression was dropped in F50 because the idea would be expressed in another way in the very next paragraph; but it confirms the interpretation I have given to the word in the present passage.

In addition F50 grants to the general the authority to explain the doubts that may arise in connection with our Institute "as comprised in this Formula." The specific approval of the Formula made it pontifical law, which can only be interpreted by the Holy See, unless—as happens in this case—someone is granted power to interpret it.

3. The Council

Two kinds of questions are distinguished: matters of major and of lesser importance.

a. Matters of Major Importance

> "The council, which must necessarily be convoked to
> establish or change the Constitutions and for other matters
> of more than ordinary importance, such as the alienation or
> dissolution of houses and colleges once erected, should be
> understood (according to the explanation in our Constitu-
> tions) to be the greater part of the entire professed Society
> which can be summoned without grave inconvenience by the
> superior general."

F39 and F40 merely stated: "matters of major importance and long-lasting." F50 is more specific. In the first place it added: "to establish or change the Constitutions" (which F39 and F40 included in the previous

51 This is the meaning given to the word in the existing English translation [editor's note].

paragraph, as we have seen), and then "for other matters of more than ordinary importance" (*graviora* in Latin), such as the alienation or dissolution of houses and colleges.

Paul III had granted permission, in the bull "Iniunctum nobis" of 1544, to change the Constitutions. But both Ignatius and Polanco feared that such an ample concession might be used to change them "for the worse" and sought to safeguard some points of the Constitutions by making them immutable, either in the bull of approval itself or in a separate papal document.[52]

Alienation does not have the restricted meaning of sale, but the larger one of transfer into other hands.

"Other matters of more than ordinary importance" is stated generally. "Long-lasting" is not added, as in F39 and F40, because, as the Constitutions explain, some matters, even though not "long-lasting," may be of sufficient importance to make a general congregation necessary; and on the contrary, the fact that a matter is "long-lasting" may not be enough (to summon a general congregation).[53]

The council must be convoked to resolve these issues.[54] This council "should be understood . . . to be the greater part of the entire professed Society which can be summoned without grave inconvenience by the superior general." The adjective "professed" was added by F50. When F39 and F40 were written there were no coadjutors, and the scholastics were not yet considered to be actual members of the Society.[55] Instead of "without grave inconvenience," those two first drafts merely had "conveniently" (*commode*), a word that can be interpreted very loosely. But the inconvenience in mind is not that of the superior general but that of the professed "who may not be able to come without grave inconvenience."[56]

The text refers to the Constitutions for further details. They, in fact, do develop this topic and expound the prescriptions of the Formula in chapters 2 to 7 of Part VIII.

---

52 *Dubiorum Series Tertia*: MI Const I 312; *Series Quarta*, nn. 59 and 60: ibid 331.
53 Cf. Const P. VIII, ch. 2 C [681]; *Dubiorum Series Tertia*: MI Const I 298; *Series Quarta*, n. 11: ibid 321.
54 Cf. Const P. VIII, ch. 2, n. 2, C [680-681].
55 Cf. *Dubiorum Series Tertia*, n. 8: MI Const I 299; *Series Quarta*, n. 14: ibid 322.
56 *Dubiorum Series Quarta*, n. 12: MI Const I 322; cf. *Series Tertia*, n. 6: ibid 299.

b. Matters of Lesser Importance

"In other matters which are of lesser importance, the same general, aided by counsel from his brethren to the extent that he will deem fitting, shall have the full right personally to order and command whatever he judges in the Lord to pertain to the glory of God and the common good, as will be explained in the Constitutions."

This paragraph differs remarkably from the formulation in F39 and F40, which declared: "in matters of lesser importance and not long-lasting, the council should be understood to be all those who happen to be present in the superior's place of residence; but the superior will have full right to command."[57]

The first part of the above paragraph can be interpreted in two ways. First: all those who happen to be present in the superior's place of residence, gathered in a local congregation or chapter, shall decide on these matters collegially. Second: all those who happen to be present at the superior's place of residence can be occasional consultors and he is free to consult them on these matters, with no obligation to summon the whole Society.

The obvious meaning is the former, and this is how some have understood it.[58] But there are powerful reasons to think that the latter interpretation reflects Ignatius' thinking better. We know that the Formula originated in the deliberations held by our Fathers in the spring of 1539. On June 11 of that year, when discussing the specific issue of admissions and dismissals, they took the following resolution or "determination": "the superior should get the opinion of some of his congregation, those he considers to be more knowledgeable as regards these admissions and dismissals; having done this, he shall pray over it and decide whatever he might judge to be more convenient for the glory of God and the good of his community (or congregation); it is up to him, and him alone, to judge freely whether the man should be admitted or not, and the same about dismissals."[59] Later on, when F50 was being prepared, Polanco asked Ignatius whether those present should be called together on these less

---

57 F39 read "ejecutar y mandar" (to execute and command). F40 omitted "ejecutar," perhaps to avoid giving the impression that the general should be a mere executor of the council's decisions.

58 Juan Mariana, S.J., for instance in his *Discurso de las enfermedades de la Compañía* (Madrid 1768), ch. 10, 149.

59 MI Const I 13, n. 16.

important matters, and the majority view followed; Ignatius replied in the negative and added: "Nevertheless, if it does happen that the superior wishes to know what the others feel, he is free to do so and then take the decision by himself, according to his own conscience."[60] This, in fact, is the method he followed and which he left in writing in a remarkable "determinatio antiqua."[61]

This is also the method prescribed in this passage of F50. There are two stages. First, the superior general (and the norm applies to all superiors) is "aided by counsel from his brethren to the extent that he will deem fitting," or as Ignatius put it in yet another reply to Polanco, "he may consult all or some of the house, jointly or separately, as he pleases."[62] Then comes the second stage: having ascertained the opinion of his brethren, he takes the final decision: he "shall have the full right personally to order and command whatever he judges in the Lord to pertain to the glory of God and the common good."

"Personally," by himself, not collegially. It conveys the "ipse solus" of the 1539 "determinatio."

"To order" was added by F50. "To command" may have to be understood of formal commands, in the strict sense of the word, whereas "to order" may refer to the ordinary business of government. The Constitutions are referred to once again; they mainly define the authority of the superior general in chapter 3 of Part IX.

---

60 *Dubiorum Series Tertia:* MI Const I 299; *Series Quarta,* n. 10: ibid 321.
61 MI Const I 210, n. 23.
62 *Dubiorum Series Quarta,* n. 89: MI Const I 336-337.

THE SECOND CHAPTER:
THE VOW OF OBEDIENCE TO THE POPE

As I have already remarked, not only does the Society imitate the Apostles in their evangelizing work but, just as they were sent by Christ, in the same way members of the Society are sent by the vicar of Christ on earth. The better to respond to this aspect of its vocation, the Society vows obedience to the vicar of Christ.

The chapter is divided into two parts: the vow, and how it is to be observed.

I. THE VOW

The first part can be divided further into three main points: the spirit of the vow, the reasons for making it, and its modality.

1. The Spirit of the Vow

> "All who make the profession in this Society should understand at the time, and furthermore keep in mind as long as they live, that this entire Society and the individual members who make their profession in it are campaigning for God under faithful obedience to His Holiness Pope Paul III and his successors in the Roman pontificate."

Chapter 2 is not formulated as an enunciation or spelling out of principles or norms. Like chapter 1, it too is addressed to "all who make the profession in this Society." To them alone because only the professed make the vow of obedience to the pope. F39 and F40 used the word "all" because the Society that was envisaged at the time comprised only the professed. In chapter 1 they were exhorted to keep the Institute, which is a pathway to God, before their eyes while they lived; in the same way they are exhorted now not only to "understand at the time" of making their profession (literally, on the threshold of their profession) but "furthermore keep in mind as long as they live" this peculiar aspect, this missionary dimension of the Institute. Here too the "always" of the first two drafts was changed into "as long as they live" and also for the same reason: to avoid a misinterpretation, as though we should be thinking of this all the time, without interruption.[1]

Before speaking of the vow as such, the text states the principle that led to it and which constitutes its spirit as it were, namely: that "this entire Society and the individual members who make their profession in it are campaigning for God under faithful obedience to His Holiness the pope." The distinction between "this entire Society and the individual members" can be read as indicating that it is not yet referring to the obligation that binds the professed in virtue of his special vow but to a wider obligation affecting the Society as such. The Society is "campaigning for God," i.e., lives its religious commitment "under faithful obedience" to the pope. At that time religious were not considered to be subject to the pope in virtue of the common vow of obedience, as to the highest superior of all religious orders, but only in virtue of his universal jurisdiction as the supreme shepherd of the Church. Hence, to say that the whole Society lives its religious commitment under obedience to the pope is tantamount to stating a peculiar kind of dependence, not common to the other religious orders.

It was this peculiar dependence that led to the vow of special obedience.

There are two vows from the historical point of view: those of Montmartre and those of Rome. By the "papal clause" of the Montmartre vows the first Fathers bound themselves to report to the pope so that he might determine their field of apostolate. As I have recalled on more than one occasion, Paul III did not assign one single field of apostolate to the whole group. Instead, he began to send them individually and thus reserved to himself these "missions" or the sending of each individual to various fields of evangelical work. The more generously and perfectly to respond to the situation thus created by the pope—which our Fathers considered a great blessing of the Lord[2]—they resolved that whoever joined the Society should make the vow of going wherever the pope might send him. This was their very first decision, taken on May 3, 1539, and confirmed the next day.[3]

These two phases seem to be reflected in this passage of the Formula. The Society campaigns under faithful obedience to the pope from the very moment that he reserved the "missions" to himself, and this is why the vow became obligatory. F39 put the connection more clearly: "the Society and

1   *Dubiorum Series Tertia:* MI Const I 300; *Series Quarta:* n. 16: ibid 322.
2   Cf. Favre in MI FontNarr I 42.
3   MI Const I 10, n. 1.

each one of its members campaign for God under faithful obedience to His Holiness Pope Paul III, and so subject is it to the government and divine authority of the vicar of Christ that . . . it binds itself by vow to obey him."

2. Reasons for Taking the Vow

> "The Gospel does indeed teach us, and we know from orthodox faith and firmly hold, that all of Christ's faithful are subject to the Roman pontiff as their head and as the vicar of Christ. Yet for the sake of greater devotion in obedience to the Apostolic See, of greater abnegation of our own wills, and of surer direction from the Holy Spirit . . ."

This is where the present chapter has undergone the most changes. F39 had advanced no reasons. The unspoken reason was, I believe, the one I have mentioned: the desire to respond in the best possible way to the kind of situation created by the pope's reserving the missions to himself. But Cardinal Ghinucci's objection—that the vow was superfluous because every Christian, and more so the clergy, was obliged to obey the pope— made it necessary to add "some reasons" in F40, namely, "The Gospel does teach us, and we know from our orthodox faith and firmly hold, that all of Christ's faithful are subject to the Roman pontiff . . . yet for the sake of the greater humility of our Society and the perfect abnegation of each one of us and the abnegation of our wills . . ."

When F50 was being prepared, Polanco felt that these reasons might be undestood as implying that we considered ourselves perfectly mortified, and he suggested the present wording. Ignatius agreed at first, but later on wondered "whether it would be proper to question the vow"[4]—a cryptic expression that seems to mean: "whether it would be proper to justify the vow at all." Polanco's suggestion was nonetheless eventually accepted: "for the sake of greater devotion in obedience to the Apostolic See, of greater [not "perfect"] abnegation of our own wills, and of surer direction from the Holy Spirit."

It was to obtain a surer direction from the Holy Spirit that our Fathers placed themselves in the pope's hands: "to avoid erring in the way of the Lord."[5] Devotion and obedience to the Apostolic See persuaded them to take the vow themselves and prescribe it for others. As for the last reason, the second part of this chapter will show how much abnegation and indifference are required for the faithful observance of this vow.

---

4 *Dubiorum Series Tertia*: l.c. 301; *Series Quarta:* ibid n. 22, 323.
5 Const P. VII, ch. 1, B [605].

3. Modality of the Vow

> "We have judged it to be extremely profitable if each one
> of us and all those who may make the same profession in
> the future would, in addition to the ordinary bond of the
> three vows, be bound by a special vow to carry out, without
> subterfuge or excuse and at once (as far as in us lies),
> whatever the present and future Roman pontiffs may order
> pertaining to the progress of souls and the propagation of
> the faith, and to go to whatsoever provinces they may
> choose to send us, whether they decide to send us among
> the Turks or any other infidels, even those who live in the
> regions called the Indies, or among any heretics or schismat-
> ics or any of the faithful."

There are three ideas here: those who are to make the vow; that it is
a special vow; and the scope or object of the vow.

a. Who Make the Vow

"Each one of us and all those who may make the same profession in
the future." This profession is the solemn one, which alone was called by
this name at the time. The coadjutors—according to what Paul III had
established in 1546 in his first approval and confirmed in F50—were to
take simple and perpetual vows, but conditioned as regards perpetuity: "as
long as the superior general thinks that they should be retained in the
Society." (A special vow of obedience to the pope that may cease to bind
without the pope's own intervention is unthinkable.)

b. It Is a Special Vow

Those who make the profession in the Society must, "in addition to the
ordinary bond of the three vows," make "a special vow." The vows of
chastity, poverty, and obedience mentioned in chapter 1 are common to all
religious. This fourth vow is peculiar to the professed of the Society, who
alone take it.

But what is the need for this special vow? All the faithful are obliged
to obey the pope as the head of the Church and vicar of Christ; every
religious is bound to obey him in virtue of the common vow of obedience
as the first superior of every religious institute. True, this obligation was
not known at the time and it was not beyond dispute until the 1917 Code
of Canon Law. Hence it may be argued: now, however, when this doctrine

is official teaching,[6] would not the common vow of obedience suffice, without the need of a special vow? It may be so in strict law. But, first of all, their formal object is different. The common vow binds religious to obey the pope inasmuch as he is the first superior of all religious. The Society's professed bind themselves to obey him "circa missiones" because the pope has reserved these "missions" to himself; the vow would bind them even if the pope were not their first religious superior.

But the spiritual aspect of the vow is more important than the merely juridical. By reserving the missions to himself, the pope bound the Society to the vicar of Christ (and hence to Christ Himself) more immediately and intimately. The best way we have to respond to this initiative of the pope —"a singular favor from God" (Favre), "our principle and main foundation" (Ignatius)—is to make a special vow of obedience to the pope that may foster and confirm our own devotion to the Apostolic See and bear testimony to it before the faithful. Take away this special vow and the Society will have lost one of its most characteristic traits, one that has attracted the attacks of the enemies of the Church and the approval of her more faithful children.

c. The Object of the Vow

It is described in the words that follow: to carry out whatever the pope may order pertaining to the progress of souls and the propagation of the faith and to go to whatsoever region he may choose to send us.

This question has often been discussed, even recently. Some stretch the object of the vow to the entire field of obedience; others restrict it just to the "missions."

To avoid confusion, note that we are not here dealing with the spirit of the vow—already dealt with—but rather with its object, or the obligation it imposes, the interpretation of which ought always to be strict.

The initial phrases seem to favor the former interpretation: "to carry out without subterfuge or excuse, at once . . . whatever (they) may order. . . ." But it must be noted that these words are meant to reflect the determination taken by the Fathers on May 3, 1539, and confirmed the next day, and that it concerned the missions only. It read: "Whoever joins the said congregation or company will be obliged to make an explicit vow of obedience to the supreme pontiff directly, whereby he offers to go to

---

6 Cf. 1917 Code of Canon Law, c. 499 § 1; 1983 Code, c. 590 § 2: "Individual members are also bound to obey the Supreme Pontiff as their highest superior by reason of the sacred bond of obedience."

any province or region, whether among the faithful or the infidels. . . ."[7]
In the second place, the text itself is not as wide in scope as a first reading
might lead one to believe. It contains several limitations or nuances. One
is contained in the words "pertaining to the progress of souls and the
propagation of the faith," which is a reference to the aims for which the
Society was founded. The "defense" of the faith is not mentioned. But we
must keep in mind that this word was added only in F50; it could have
been added here, too, but the original text was left unchanged, presumably
through oversight. In other words, when he makes this vow, the professed
of the Society binds himself to obey the pope in the matters that pertain to
the aims of his vocation, which is evangelization.

Another limitation or nuance is contained in the words "to go to
whatever regions they may choose to send us," which are not to be found
in F39 and were added in F40. These words would have made no sense if
the vow encompassed the entire field of obedience. The reason for adding
them could only have been to give greater precision to the object of the
vow, left somewhat vague in the previous phrase. Nadal realized this and
wrote: "the 'and' is explanatory, because this vow refers only to the
missions."[8]

This explains why the Formula, in seeking to stress the perfection of
this obedience to the pope, does not say "even though things are com-
manded which are difficult and repugnant to sensitive nature," as the
Constitutions do when urging perfect obedience,[9] but rather (already in
F39): "whether they decide to send us among the Turks or any other
infidels, even those who live in the regions called the Indies, or among any
heretics or schismatics or any of the faithful."[10] The context confirms this
interpretation.

The second part of this chapter speaks of being "prompt" (literally
"with loins girded," i.e., ready for departure), of neither seeking nor
refusing "such missions or provinces," of not carrying on negotiations with
the pope about them.

Yet another proof is to be found in the way of proceeding of the
authors of the Formula. When they put it into practice, the first Fathers
made the vow to obey the pope not in whatever he might command but

---

7   MI Const I 10, n. 1.
8   Cf. M. Ruiz Jurado, "Nadal y Polanco sobre la Fórmula del Instituto de la
    Compañía de Jesús" in AHSI 47 (1978) 237.
9   Const P. III, ch. 1, n. 23 [284].
10 F39 put it differently: "even if they decide to send us to the Turks or to the new
    world or to the Lutherans or to any other infidels whatsoever." The change made
    by F40 is easily explained. The list is now more complete and logical.

"regarding the missions contained in the bull," and the bull was "Regimini militantis," which included and approved the Formula of the Institute.[11]

Finally, an authentic interpretation of this passage of the Formula is given by Ignatius in the Constitutions: "The entire meaning of this fourth vow of obedience to the pope was and is in regard to the missions. In this manner too should be understood the bulls in which obedience is treated: in everything which the sovereign pontiff commands and wheresoever he sends one, and the like."[12]

Polanco inquired whether it might be good to add that the professed should go wherever the pope might send him "even with danger to his life," "without asking for provisions," or "without provisions for the journey." Ignatius did not think the former point needed to be mentioned. As for provisions for the journey, he replied that the Constitutions, not the Formula, was the place in which to state that they "must report to the pope, ready and willing to go in the manner His Holiness would tell them."[13] This is what was done.[14]

II. OBSERVANCE OF THE VOW

Three norms are given regarding the observance of this vow: to think it over before making it; to be always prompt; to be indifferent.

1. Reflection

> "Therefore before those who will come to us take this
> burden upon their shoulders, they should ponder long and
> seriously, as the Lord has counseled, whether they possess
> among their resources enough spiritual capital to complete
> this tower; that is, whether the Holy Spirit who moves them
> is offering them so much grace that with His aid they have
> hope of bearing the weight of this vocation."

The scriptural reference is to the Lord's words in Luke: "Which of you, intending to build a tower, would not first sit down and work out the cost to see if he had enough to complete it? Otherwise, if he laid the foundation and then found himself unable to finish the work, the onlookers would all

---

11 MI Const I 67-68.
12 Const P. V, ch. 3, C [529].
13 *Dubiorum Series Tertia:* l.c. 301-302; *Series Quarta,* n. 23: ibid 324.
14 Const P. VII, ch. 1, n. 3 [609]; cf. P. VI, ch. 2, n. 13 [573].

start making fun of him and saying, 'Here is a man who started to build and was unable to finish.'"[15]

In our case the tower means the obligations imposed by the vow, i.e. to carry out, without subterfuge or excuse, whatever the pope may order us regarding the progress of souls and the propagation of the faith and to go to whatever part of the world he may send us. The spiritual capital required to complete this tower is the grace of the Holy Spirit. The Holy Spirit is the one who moves or impels them to consecrate themselves to God. Through spiritual discernment they must see whether He moves them to this particular kind of consecrated life, to "campaign for God in this Society"; whether the Holy Spirit "is offering them so much grace that, with His aid," they can reasonably expect to be able to bear "the weight of this vocation." This offer of grace will be noticed in the courage and strength and consolations that make it all easy and remove all obstacles.[16] This will give them hope that they will be able to bear this burden, not indeed trusting in their own strength but relying solely on the help of the Holy Spirit: "with His aid."

2. *Availability*

> "Then, after they have enlisted through the inspiration of
> the Lord in this militia of Christ, they ought to be prompt
> in carrying out this obligation which is so great, being clad
> for battle day and night."

The consideration by the mind ought to be followed by promptitude of the will.

"They have enlisted through the inspiration of the Lord" because He alone calls to the religious life and to the Society.[17]

"This militia of Christ," and similar expressions, "to serve as a soldier of God," "campaigning for God," are frequent in patristic and medieval literature when referring to God's service.[18]

"Prompt" and "clad for battle day and night" are meant to translate the Latin "die noctuque succinti lumbos"—with loins girded day and night, a biblical expression repeated by the classics of spirituality. It means readiness to start on a journey. This is how the Israelites were instructed to eat the paschal lamb[19] and how the Lord wants us to await His second

---

15 Lk 14:27-30.
16 SpEx 315.
17 Cf. Const P. III, ch. 1, n. 1 [243].
18 Cf. *Dictionnaire de Spiritualité*, vol. 10, col. 1210-1226.
19 Ex 12:11.

coming.[20] Horace calls those walking faster than himself: "altius prae-cincti."[21] Ignatius uses another metaphor in one of his letters: "The Society, according to its Institute, must, so to speak, have one foot on the road, ready to hasten from one place to another."[22] It is this mobility and availability proper to the Society which has determined so many of its characteristics: the exclusion of choir and of the care of both parishes and religious communities. . . .[23]

"In carrying out this obligation which is so great" is a legitimate translation of "tam grandis debiti solutionem": literally, "the payment of so great a debt."

3. Indifference

> "However, to forestall among us any ambition for such missions or provinces, or any refusal of them, all our members should have this understanding: they should not either by themselves or through someone else carry on negotiations with the Roman pontiff about such missions, but leave all this care to God and to the pope himself as His vicar, and to the superior general of the Society. Indeed, the general too, just like the rest, should not treat with the said pontiff about himself being sent or not, unless after advice from the Society."

This paragraph is the result of the following resolution taken by the first Fathers on May 3, 1539: "Should anyone of this congregation desire to go to one particular region rather than another, whether of the faithful or the infidels, he must not have recourse to the supreme pontiff directly or indirectly, personally or through others, in order that the pope may send him; rather, he will submit to the judgment of the congregation or its superior, disclosing this desire or opinion of his to the former or the latter, ready to do whatever they may order him."[24]

It goes without saying that anyone who makes this special vow regarding the missions cannot refuse them. But more is demanded of him here: he cannot "ambition" them. This ban is not to be understood of the internal act of desiring them but of the external acts, the negotiations set

---

20 Lk 12:35.
21 Q. Horatius Flaccus, *Sat* I 5.
22 To Mateo Sebastián de Morano, February 22, 1549: MI Epp II 346 (Young p. 187).
23 Const P. VI, ch. 3, nn. 4-6 [586-589].
24 MI Const I 11, n. 7.

in motion with the purpose of being sent. The Constitutions use the words "to arrange or try to arrange."

To forestall any such possibility comes the addition: "All our members should have this understanding: they should not either by themselves or through someone else carry on negotiations with the Roman pontiff about such missions." F39 and F40 had stated: "all should profess" instead of "all should understand." This was changed presumably because the word "profess" lent itself to misunderstanding, as though it meant taking a vow.[25]

The words "either by themselves or through someone else" are also the result of a change. Both F39 and F40 stated: "either directly or indirectly." Polanco expressed misgivings about the word "indirectly," as he had earlier on about the words "without excuse." It could well happen on some occasion that the one appointed by the pope for a mission fell sick or felt he was not sufficiently qualified, and on the other hand he could not contact the superior general, or the superior general could not refer the matter to the pope, and so forth. Ignatius did not want the words "without excuse" to be removed, but relented about "indirectly."[26] Frankly, however, I do not see any difference between the previous "directly or indirectly" and the present "by themselves or through someone else," unless the former may have to be understood as meaning that one cannot treat with the pope either about the mission itself (to be sent or not) or the circumstances, favorable or unfavorable, in which he finds himself.

Far from treating with the pope regarding these missions, those concerned must "leave all this care to God, and to the pope himself as His vicar, and to the superior general of the Society." It is an attitude of abandonment of self: giving up the care or disposal of oneself. The Constitutions put it thus: "In this matter the Society has subjected its own judgment and desire to that of Christ our Lord and His vicar."[27]

When the text declares: "leave all this care to God," as in other Ignatian writings the word God signifies Christ. This is confirmed by the words that follow: "and to the pope as *His* Vicar," as well as by the parallel passage of the Constitutions just quoted. "All this care" must be left first to God and then to the Roman pontiff, but inasmuch as he is Christ's vicar, who not only takes the place of Christ in the Church's universal government ("feed my sheep"),[28] but also has reserved to himself the missions of the professed of the Society, to send them personally, as Christ sent His

25 Cf. *Dubiorum Series Tertia:* l.c. 302.
26 *Dubiorum Series Tertia:* l.c. 300; *Series Quarta,* n. 17: ibid 322.
27 Const P. VII, ch. 1, n. 2 [606].
28 Jn 21:5.

Apostles. "All this care" is next left to the superior of the Society: as Ignatius explained in an answer to Polanco, the superior is empowered to treat directly with the pope both about sending a Jesuit and about recalling those who have been sent.[29]

But the superior general, too, like everyone else, is forbidden to treat with the pope about being sent himself, whether it be for or against. In his case, however, one condition is given: "unless after advice from the Society." It can happen, in fact, that the pope may not know certain facts and if he knew them he would not send him,[30] and there is no one above the superior general to supply the information. But what does "Society" actually mean here? Nadal thinks it is the general congregation or the professed who reside with the general.[31] But since the four assistants are there to represent the Society in the care to be taken of the person and government of the general, this condition of the Formula would be observed if the general followed their advice.

---

29 *Dubiorum Series Tertia:* l.c. 301; *Series Quarta,* n. 20: ibid 323.
30 Const P. VII, ch. 1, C [607].
31 Cf. M.Ruiz Jurado, "Nadal y Polanco....", art. quoted in note 8, 237.

THE THIRD CHAPTER:
THE VOW OF OBEDIENCE
TO THE SUPERIOR OF THE SOCIETY

Two vows of obedience are made in the Society: one is common to all religious, that of obedience to superiors; and the other, special, of obedience to the pope. Having discussed the latter, a word had to be said about the former. This clearly defines the two areas of obedience existing in the Society: a "missionary" obedience, involved in the fourth vow of the professed, and a "corporative" obedience, as some authors have called it, which is the object of this vow of obedience to superiors.[1]

The chapter can be divided into three parts or topics: the vow of obedience, the election and authority of the superior, and the manner of exercising authority and obedience.

I. THE VOW

> "All should likewise vow that in all matters that concern the
> observance of this Rule they will be obedient to the one put
> in charge of the Society."

"All" because the content of this chapter is applicable to all the members of the Society, even though the Formula is generally addressed to the professed. Only chapter 4 speaks of the scholastics and there is a reference to the coadjutors right at the end.

The object or matter of the vow is to obey the superior general of the Society (and all those who may have received authority from him) in whatever concerns the observance of this Rule. This is where the Formula is called the Rule or fundamental law of the Society, which general congregations later confirmed.

---

1 Cf. L. Mendizábal, "Sentido íntimo de la obediencia ignaciana," in *Manresa* 37 (1965) 53-76; J. Iturrioz, "Dos lineas de obediencia en la Compañía de Jesús," in *Manresa* 43 (1971) 59-78.

For the rest, there is nothing but a repetition of common doctrine. The vow of obedience binds one to obey only the commands of the superior that are "according to the Rule," not those that are against or beyond the Rule. The virtue of obedience, especially in the Society, goes much further: "not only in matters of obligation but also in the others, even though nothing else is perceived except the indication of the superior's will without an express command . . . in all the things into which obedience can with charity be extended."[2]

Polanco feared that the words "in all matters that concern the observance of this Rule" could lead to the assumption that any deviation from obedience would entail a mortal sin on account of the vow. Ignatius did not want these words to be changed or suppressed, but he suggested that a declaration should be made in the Constitutions to the effect that in the Society there exists no obligation binding under pain of sin, except if and when the superior issues an order in virtue of obedience or in the name of Christ.[3] This was actually done.[4]

II. ELECTION AND AUTHORITY OF THE SUPERIOR GENERAL

These two paragraphs were added in F50 and did not exist in either F39 or F40. They are again the result of a question by Polanco to Ignatius as to whether something should be added about this in the Formula. Ignatius agreed that something could be said, but in rather general terms, leaving the details for the Constitutions.[5] Chapter 1 might have been a more suitable place, since both the points are touched upon there: election and authority.

1. Election

> "He should be the best qualified for this office and will be elected by a majority of votes (as will be explained in the Constitutions)."

Only two points are made: the election should be by a majority of votes, and the most suitable should be elected. Reference is then made to

---

2 Const P. VI, ch. 1, n. 1 [547].
3 *Dubiorum Series Tertia:* MI Const I 302; *Series Quarta,* n. 25: ibid 324.
4 Const P. VI; ch. 5 [602].
5 Cf. *Dubiorum Series Tertia:* l.c. 303; *Series Quarta,* nn. 26-27: ibid 324.

the Constitutions, which discuss the election of the general in chapter 6 of Part VIII[6] and the qualities of the general in chapter 2 of Part IX.[7]

2. Authority

> "He should possess all the authority and power over the Society which are useful for its good administration, correction, and government."

The Constitutions put it this way: "It is judged altogether proper for the good government of the Society that the superior general should have complete authority over it, in order to build it up."[8] And there follows a more detailed description of the general's powers.[9]

If we were to draw a distinction between "administration" and "government" we might say that administration refers to business matters, and government to persons, though it can also have a wider meaning. "Correction" could refer to coercive power. Polanco did ask Ignatius if the Formula should say something about penalties. Ignatius thought the Constitutions would be a better place.[10] This word, correction, might have been meant as an implicit reference.

III. HOW TO EXERCISE AUTHORITY AND PRACTICE OBEDIENCE

1. How to Exercise Authority

What the general should command is described first, and then the manner in which he should exercise that authority.

a. What He Should Command

> "He should issue the commands which he knows to be opportune for achieving the end set before him by God and the Society."

---

6 Const P. VIII, ch. 6 [694-710].
7 Const P. IX, ch. 2 [723-735].
8 Const P. IX, ch. 3, n. 1 [736].
9 Const P. IX, ch. 3 [736-765].
10 *Dubiorum Series Tertia:* l.c. 311; *Series Quarta,* n. 55: ibid 330. But in fact neither do the Constitutions contain what could be called a penal code, like those of other religious orders. Correction and penances for faults are left to the superior's discretion. Cf. Const P. III, ch. 1, n. 15 N [269-270]; P. IX, ch. 3, n. 11 [754].

What is this end, set before the general by God and the Society? It is spelled out in the Constitutions: "the good government, preservation, and development [or growth] of the whole body of the Society,"[11] "to govern the whole body of the Society in such a manner that through the divine grace it may be preserved and developed in its well-being and manner of proceeding for glory to God our Lord."[12] We should note that the topic of Part X of the Constitutions is precisely "how the whole body of the Society can be preserved and developed in its well-being." This Part will show the general what is helpful for the end the Society has set before him.

b. How He Should Command

"In his superiorship he should be ever mindful of the kindness, meekness, and charity of Christ and of the pattern set by Peter and Paul, a norm which both he and the aforementioned council should keep constantly in view."

The first words are somewhat obscure in the original Latin. Ribadeneira's translation (which we follow) seems to interpret them correctly. Nadal interpreted them as follows in one of his writings: "mindful of the meekness, kindness, and charity exhibited by Christ, St. Peter, and St. Paul."[13] This reading is possible but less natural and, besides, places Christ on the same level as Peter and Paul.

To illustrate the meekness, kindness, and charity of Christ one would have to quote the Gospels almost in full. This is what impresses most in the image of Christ they portray. Take, for instance, the discourse of the Last Supper. Suffice it to quote St. Peter's summing up when he said that Jesus "went about doing good and curing all who had fallen into the power of the devil."[14] "He was insulted and did not retaliate with insults; when he was tortured he made no threats but put his trust in the righteous judge. . . . 'Through his wounds you have been healed.'"[15] There is also the first song of the servant of Yahweh.[16]

Of "the pattern set by Peter and Paul" let me say that St. Gregory the Great too presents them as models of the pastors of the Church in his famous *Regula Pastoralis.*[17]

---

11 Const P. IX, ch. 1 [719].
12 Const P. IX, ch. 6, n. 1 [789].
13 MHSI Nadal IV 515.
14 Acts 10:38.
15 1 Pt 2:23-25.
16 Is 42:1-4.
17 St. Gregory, *Regula pastoralis* ch. 6.

It is quite remarkable that the Formula does not consider any other qualities except meekness, kindness, and charity. It is the same in the Constitutions: "Further help will be found in his having his method of commanding well thought out and organized,[18] through his endeavoring to maintain obedience in the subjects in such a manner that the superior on his part uses all the love and modesty and charity possible in our Lord, so that the subjects can dispose themselves to have always toward their superiors greater love than fear, even though both are useful at times. He can also do this . . . by going along with them to some extent and sympathizing with them when this, it seems, could be more expedient."[19] The last words (from "the superior on his part uses all the love . . .") are in Ignatius' own hand. Love, modesty, and charity, however, are not synonymous with permissiveness. The superior has to blend severity with kindness[20] and occasionally resort to correction, which too is to be done "with love and gentleness."[21]

2. Recommendation on the Teaching of Catechism

F39 and F40 had the following paragraph here: "[The superior general and his council should] particularly . . . hold esteemed the instruction of children and the unlettered in the Christian doctrine of the Ten Commandments and other similar rudiments, whatever will seem suitable to them in accordance with the circumstances of persons, places, and times. For it is very necessary that the superior and the council give this matter the most diligent attention, since the edifice of faith cannot arise among our fellowmen without a foundation and since there is danger that as one becomes more learned he may disregard this occupation, less prestigious at first glance, when none in fact is more fruitful, either for the neighbor to be edified or for Ours to discharge occupations that combine both humility and charity."

This paragraph was dropped in F50. Polanco asked Ignatius if the teaching of Christian doctrine should be urged more than other ministries such as preaching and hearing confessions. Ignatius replied that "one should not be more recommended than another, but everything should be done as thought best."[22] The same reason had led to the cancellation of the word "nominatim" when listing the ministries of the Society. This, however,

---

18 Or perhaps better: thoughtful and well-ordered [editor's note].
19 Const P. VIII, ch. 1, G [667].
20 Const P. IX, ch. 2, n. 4 [727].
21 Const P. III, ch. 1, N [270].
22 *Dubiorum Series Tertia:* l.c. 304; *Series Quarta* n. 31: ibid. 325.

does not mean that Ignatius lost in any way the esteem he had for this ministry. He was a catechist all his life. He had it mentioned in the profession, and the declaration explaining it contains the substance of the reasons advanced in this paragraph.[23]

3. How to Practice Obedience

> "Assuredly, too, because of the great value of good order and for the sake of the constant practice of humility, never sufficiently praised, the individual subjects should not only be obliged to obey the general in all matters pertaining to the Society's Institute but also to recognize and properly venerate Christ as present in him."

Two ideas are indicated: the reason for obeying, and the spirit that ought to inspire obedience.

Two reasons are given to urge obedience. First, "the great value of good order." Authority is the formal element of an organized corporation or society. Without authority it would be a disorganized and dispersed crowd. But this would also be the case if authority were not effective or the subjects did not submit to it.

The second reason is "the constant practice of humility, never sufficiently praised." There can be no obedience without humility. The submission implied in obedience requires lowering in order to "submit." Constant submission through obedience entails constant practice of humility, never sufficiently praised because ever since Adam's sin man's tendency is to self-exaltation, to love of self to the point of forgetting God. Only through humility and submission will he reverse this process and love God to the point of forgetting self.

I have already pointed out what is the object or matter of the vow of obedience. Much the same is repeated now: all should be obliged "to obey the general in all matters pertaining to the Society's Institute," "as comprised within this Formula."

But it is not enough to obey the general: obedience is to be enlightened by supernatural light, recognizing and venerating 'Christ present in him." After his resurrection, Christ is present in the world in manifold ways, not to speak of His real presence in the Eucharist. He is present as often as His disciples gather together in his name.[24] He is present in the person of the minister of the sacraments: "if Peter baptizes, it is Christ who

23 Const P. V, ch. 3, B [528].
24 Mt 18:20.

baptizes." He is present in the preaching of the Apostles: "anyone who listens to you, listens to me."[25] He is present in the sick, the hungry, the thirsty, those in prison or in need.[26] Monastic tradition has always considered the superior as representative of Christ, from whom he has received his authority.[27] St. Benedict writes in his Rule: "we believe that the abbot takes Christ's place in the monastery."[28] "We believe" ("creditur" in Latin) is not simply "we think" or "imagine" but much more. We could almost translate "we profess." This may well be the most often repeated idea in the Ignatian Constitutions: the superior takes the place of Christ.[29] The Formula, however, goes beyond a cold intellectual recognition; it wants it to be accompanied by the veneration due to Christ, present in the superior.[30] We venerate Christ present in the Eucharist. The manner of this presence is certainly different, but Christ is one and the same in both cases.

25 Lk 10:16.
26 Mt 25:35.
27 Cf. L. Mendizábal, "Riqueza eclesial y teológica de la obediencia religiosa," in *Manresa* 36 (1964) 283-307.
28 St. Benedict, *Regula*, ch. 2, 2; ch. 62, 13.
29 Cf. Exam ch. 4, n. 29 [84]; Const P. III, ch. 1, n. 23 [284]; P. IV, ch. 4, n. 3 [342]; ch. 10, n. 5 [424]; P. VI, ch. 1, n. 1 [657]; P. VII, ch. 2, n. 1 [618]; P. IX, ch. 3, n. 10 [765].
30 Cf. Const P. VI, ch. 1, n. 2 [551].

THE FOURTH CHAPTER:
THE VOW OF POVERTY

This chapter also is clearly divided into two parts: the poverty of the Society, and the exception made in the case of the scholastics.

I. THE POVERTY OF THE SOCIETY

This first paragraph contains the reasons for the kind of poverty professed by the Society (the protasis in the Latin text), and it then explains its content, which is the matter and object of the vow (the apodosis).

1. The Reasons

> "From experience we have learned that a life removed as far as possible from all contagion of avarice and as like as possible to evangelical poverty is more gratifying, more undefiled, and more suitable for the edification of our fellowmen. We likewise know that our Lord Jesus Christ will supply to His servants who are seeking only the kingdom of God what is necessary for food and clothing."

The basic reason is the life ideal that fired Ignatius and his companions: "a life removed as far as possible from all contagion of avarice and as like as possible to evangelical poverty."

Avarice is a "contagious" virus. The craving to possess is not quenched by satisfaction; on the contrary, that only feeds the craving. The first step in Satan's tactics is "to covet riches"; this leads to the second and third steps. The only effective preventive remedy (prophylaxis) is the one used against contagious diseases: get as far away as possible from any danger of contagion, which the possession of earthly goods invariably implies.

Opposed to avarice is evangelical poverty. But which evangelical poverty does Ignatius have in mind? The Gospel reports that during his hidden life Jesus earned his livelihood working as a poor artisan. It also tells us that during his public life he had nowhere to lay his head[1] and lived on alms alone.[2] It is this second type of poverty that, according to Matthew, Jesus gave to his Apostles as a norm when He sent them on their apostolic mission: you received without charge, give without charge; take neither gold nor silver nor copper for your purses, for the workman deserves his keep.[3] There is a third manner of poverty in the New Testament that can rightly be called evangelical because it was the result of the preaching of the Gospel: that of the early Christian community in Jerusalem, whereby the Christians gave up private property and possessed everything in common.[4]

The context here implies that the poverty it calls evangelical is that of the public life of Jesus and the missionary life of the Apostles. This is confirmed by the Deliberation on Poverty: one of the reasons put forward for embracing poverty is that "by taking it for himself our common Lord taught it to his dear Apostles and disciples when he sent them to preach."[5] The reference to Matthew 10 is clear.

This life ideal, removed as far as possible from all avarice and as like as possible to evangelical poverty, is not conceived in an abstract sort of way, but is the fruit of actual experience, a spiritual experience at that, "before God our Lord," to use a phrase often repeated in the Constitutions. This experience taught the first Fathers that such a life of poverty is "more gratifying, more undefiled, and more suitable for the edification of our fellowmen."

The world believes that the greater the riches, the happier the life. Experience (and not only that of the first Jesuits) proves that the contrary is true. Poverty frees a person from preoccupation with material affairs and helps him to live with total trust in God's Providence. It is also more "undefiled" because the more immune to the contagion of avarice. "One lives more oblivious to all earthly satisfaction," as Ignatius put it in the Deliberation on Poverty.[6] Finally, it is "more suitable for the edification of our fellowmen." "One can thus speak more freely and effectively of spiritual matters, and the good of souls is greater," adds the Deliberation on Poverty.[7] "Edification" must be understood not in the weakened, even derisory, sense that it has nowadays. Ignatius uses it with all the force of

---

1   Mt 8:20.
2   Cf. Lk 8:1-2.
3   Mt 10:8-10.
4   Cf. Acts 2:44-45; 4:32 and 36-37.
5   MI Const I 80, n. 12.
6   MI Const I 80, n. 4bis.
7   Ibid n. 7.

its original meaning (which is also the Pauline meaning), of building up a person's spiritual edifice, his or her salvation and perfection.

There is further, in the evangelically poor life conceived by Ignatius and his companions, a lived experience of faith in God's word: "We likewise know that our Lord Jesus Christ will supply to His servants who are seeking only the kingdom of God what is necessary for food and clothing." This is, of course, an implicit quotation of Matthew's gospel: "Look at the birds in the sky. They do not sow or reap or gather into barns; yet your heavenly Father feeds them. . . . Think of the flowers growing in the fields; they never have to work or spin. . . . So do not worry; do not say, 'What are we to eat? What are we to drink? How are we to be clothed?'. . . Your heavenly Father knows you need them all. Set your hearts on his kingdom first and on his righteousness, and all these other things will be given to you as well."[8]

Two details are worth noting in this passage of the Formula: first, that the Lord will supply what is necessary, not what is superfluous; secondly, that he will supply it to those who seek only the kingdom of God. In the case of Jesuits this will have to be understood of seeking to establish the kingdom in others through "the defense and propagation of the faith and the progress of souls in Christian life and doctrine." Ignatius was convinced that whoever works to aid souls will not lack life's necessities. So much so that one of the reasons listed in the Deliberation on Poverty is that poverty makes us more ready and willing to give spiritual help to souls.[9] In the same vein he wrote to Gian Pietro Caraffa that, if they (the Theatines) were to serve the Lord by preaching or performing works of mercy in public, even without seeking alms, "the people would be more inclined to support them, and with much greater charity."[10]

2. The Poverty of the Society in F39 and F40

The paragraph that follows has gone through a number of changes. It will help to trace its historical evolution.

In F39 it read:

> "Our members, one and all, should vow perpetual poverty, declaring that they cannot, either individually or in common, acquire any civil right to any stable goods or any produce or fixed income for the maintenance or use of the Society. Rather let them be content to enjoy only the use of

8 Mt 6:25-35.
9 MI Const I 80, n. 8.
10 MI Epp I 116-117.

necessary things, with the owners permitting, and to receive the money and the value of things given them in order to buy necessities for themselves."

This paragraph spells out in greater detail the resolution Ignatius and his companions took on June 11, 1539: "We may receive houses with a church attached but without any right to their property so that those who give us their use may freely take them back if they so wish; furthermore, we shall have no right to claim them in court (in whatever way they might give them) against anyone whatever, even if they take them unjustly."[11]

"Civil right" is understood to mean a right to sue ("to claim in court" or "through litigation," as an Ignatian text we shall quote later puts it). It is based, as the resolution we have quoted implies, on the "right to property."

Not possessing any stable goods or fixed revenues "either individually or in common" is the characteristic of the poverty of the mendicant orders (Dominicans and Franciscans). The monks, like the early Christian community, did not own anything individually, but they did own in common. The owner of the stable goods and revenues was the monastery, and this is how some monasteries became very rich during the Middle Ages. St. Dominic and St. Francis decided to give up even this common ownership. But some goods, both stable, like the house and the church, and movable, like furniture, clothing, etc., are necessary for life. In the case of the Dominicans the order (the community, the convent) keeps both the use and the ownership of these goods; in that of the Franciscans the friars keep their use only, and the ownership goes to the Holy See unless the original owners who have given their use to the friars keep ownership for themselves. Ignatius and his companions resolved that those of the Society should be satisfied with the bare use of the things that are necessary; property continues to be in the hands of the owners who give them to us for use. The "necessary things": no distinction is made, and hence it must be understood to refer to both movable and immovable goods. They may have taken the idea from the early practice of the Capuchins.[12]

Unlike the practice in Franciscan poverty, the acceptance of money is explicitly allowed. St. Francis "firmly" forbade that in his Rule.[13] F39 permits receiving not only money but also "the price of the things presented to them." This seems to imply that it is permissible to sell the

11 MI Const I 13, n. 15.
12 Cf. Constantinus ab Aldeaseca, O.F.M.Cap., *Natura iuridica paupertatis ordinis Minorum Cappucinorum* (Rome 1943) 119-128.
13 St. Francis, *Regula*, ch. 4.

things received as alms for the necessities of life. But then, who has the ownership of that money and those things? The distinction between "having the use of the things necessary" and "receiving the money and the price of the things given to buy what is necessary" would seem to indicate that their ownwership lies with the Society. How else would it be entitled to sell the things received as alms unless it has the ownership?

In F40:

F40 merely copies this paragraph, without making any change. Except that through an oversight the copyist jumped from the "things" ("rerum") of line 12 to the "things" ("rerum") of line 15, omitting the lines in between. And so the Latin phrase that read

> sint contenti usu tantum rerum necessariarum, volentibus dominis, gaudere, et pecunia ac pretia rerum sibi donatarum ad comparanda sibi necessaria recipere

became

> sint contenti usu tantum rerum sibi donatarum ad necessaria sibi comparanda recipere.

Someone noticed that this was grammatically incorrect and changed *usu* into *usum*. But even with this correction the phrase made little sense: "let them be content with receiving the use of the things given to them to buy what is necessary." It is not the use that is received, but the things that are then used. If these things are given to buy what is necessary, one no longer has their use. This copying error had more important consequences than could be foreseen at the time, as we shall see.

3. Vacillations as Regards this Poverty (1511-1511)

Shortly after F40 was approved by the bull "Regimini militantis" of September 27, 1540, we come up against two documents that would seem to relax this poverty. The first is entitled "Foundation of a House."[14] The other is known as the "1541 Constitutions"[15] and contains the resolutions of the six first Fathers who were able to meet in Rome in the spring of that year to elect the first superior general and to make their profession. Nothing is known about the juridical character of the former; it could well be a working paper for the first meeting of the Fathers.[16] There is

14 MI Const I 61-64.
15 Ibid 34-38.
16 Many in fact consider it to have been written after the 1541 Constitutions because the editors of Monumenta place it after them. However, Schurhammer proved in 1943 that it had been copied by Antonio Estrada, who left Rome for Paris in

substantial agreement between this document and the 1541 Constitutions in what pertains to poverty.

Both documents permit a house of the Society (first document), or the church (second document), to have fixed revenues, not indeed for the maintenance of the professed (food and clothing), but for other needs, such as the church, furniture, library, medicines, postage, provisions for journeys. . . . These fixed revenues could be administered by the city council or a leading personality (according to the first document) or a "non-professed" appointed by the founder, while the Society would keep the superintendency (according to the 1541 Constitutions). The reasons advanced for having revenues are: that the Society would be better preserved; that we would not bother our benefactors so much; that, not having to beg for alms, the Fathers would have more time for spiritual things: apostolic ministries, prayer, study. . . .

In an effort to explain this apparent relaxation, some have traced it to certain interpretations of "mendicant poverty" then given by canonists. But the document "Foundation of a House" explicitly states that the Fathers were influenced as much by the monks as by the mendicants, borrowing some points from each.

If we compare this system of poverty with that established in F39 and F40, we notice this: the professed continue to have no "civil right" to any fixed revenues either individually or collectively. Here, as there, they are forbidden to have revenues for their own maintenance (food and clothing). Fixed revenues are permitted for other purposes, and even these revenues do not strictly belong to the Society. A juridical person, different from the Society, is established to hold the ownership of the fixed revenues. The document "Foundation of a House" illustrated this with an example: a hospital or hospice for pilgrims has all that is needed to look after them, while the pilgrims do not possess anything.

This does not seem to have satisfied Ignatius. When he took up the writing of the Constitutions in 1544, poverty was the very first topic he tackled. Two writings of his that reveal his thinking have been preserved: the Deliberation on Poverty[17] and the Spiritual Diary.[18] In the former he applies the Exercises' method of the "third time to make a good choice,"

February 1541. Therefore the document could not have been written after that date. Cf. G. Schurhammer, *Gesammelte Studien III* (Rome 1964) 469-470. Besides, the 1541 Constitutions make reference to it: "Start colleges in universities. See 'foundation'" (MI Const I 47, n. 42).

17 MI Const I 78-81.

18 MI Const I 86-158.

with reasons for and against.[19] He takes up and elaborates on the reasons listed in "Foundation of a House," and then lists other reasons "not to have any fixed revenue." The former, we notice, are dictated by human prudence, whereas the latter are spiritual and evangelical. During the first forty days recorded in the Spiritual Diary, he applied the Exercises' method of the "second time," "through experience of desolations and consolations and discernment of diverse spirits."[20] The communications he received from God during those days decided him to go back to the early poverty and give up any type of fixed revenue. He concluded the process on March 12 with full divine confirmation.

4. The Poverty of the Society in F50

> "Therefore our members, one and all, should vow perpetual poverty in such a manner that neither the professed, either individually or in common, nor any house or church of theirs can acquire any civil right to any produce, fixed revenues, or possessions or to the retention of any stable goods (except those which are proper for their own use and habitation); but they should instead be content with whatever is given them out of charity for the necessities of life."

The process we have just described accounts for some of the differences between F50 and the previous drafts of the Formula.

The peculiarities of the vow are more accurately stated. Not only are the professed barred from holding or acquiring any civil right to any kind of fixed revenue, either individually or in common, but they are not able even to own any of their houses or churches. It thus excludes the juridical person (house or church) thought up in 1541 as a possible owner of the revenues. It also specifies better the temporal goods that are barred to them: instead of saying "any produce or fixed revenues," it says "any produce, fixed revenues, or possessions." "Neither fixed revenues nor possessions" was precisely the term coined by the Dominicans in their general chapter of 1220 at Bologna to describe mendicant poverty and the one used by the Second Council of Lyons to describe the same.[21]

There are two other important changes as regards stable goods. The first is that only the civil right to keep them is excluded; the second, that an exception is made: "except those [stable goods] which are proper for

19 SpEx 178-183.
20 SpEx 176.
21 Council of Lyons II (1274), d. 23.

their own use and habitation."

F39 had stated very clearly that, according to the resolution of the first Fathers on June 11, 1539, the benefactors who gave goods to the Society for their use continued to hold their ownership. This was omitted in F40 through a copyist's error, leaving the question vague. When preparing F50, Polanco raised the question: Does the Society have any right to its residence, with its garden and the church? Ignatius' reply was in conformity with the original poverty: "Not insofar as it may claim it in court: but it would be good to secure a married person (family or friend) to defend it, etc."[22] Polanco then observed that, if the Society does not have the ownership of these goods (and the same would apply to any other goods received as alms), it would still be able to sell them or transfer ownership to others.[23] Two Roman canon law experts were consulted: who owns the residence and the church and the goods received as alms? If it is not the Society, can it defend them? Can it sell them? The experts' reply followed the rules of Franciscan poverty: the holder of ownership is the Holy See, the Church. The Society can defend those goods in the same way as the Friars Minor; it can sell the house on behalf of the Church. It can also sell any goods received in alms provided the benefactor has not given them to be retained but just to help towards the maintenance of the Society through their value in cash.[24] But—Polanco objected[25]—norms did not belong to the common law but to the Friars Minor's private law; if they were to be valid for the Society, this had to be explicitly stated. The extant written documents do not say anything further. Ignatius must have discussed the matter with his companions or some of them, and the solution we read in F50 was arrived at. This solution resembles rather the poverty of the Dominicans.

Even though the formulation "any civil right . . . to the retention of" is not a very happy one, the idea is nonetheless clear enough. The Society cannot own any stable goods save what is necessary or proper for its own use and habitation; but it can receive them in order to sell them and with the proceeds meet the needs of the poor both within and without the Society.[26] But who owns these goods? That is not so clear. It would seem that, since it is not the Society (which has no civil right to own them), it must be the donors. The Society does have the right to the retention of those goods "which are proper for their use and habitation." The scope of

---

22 *Dubiorum Series Tertia:* MI Const I 305: *Series Quarta,* n. 35: ibid 326.
23 *Dubiorum Series Tertia:* l.c. 306; *Series Quarta:* n. 41: l.c. 327.
24 MI Const I 351-352.
25 *Dubiorum Series Tertia:* l.c. 306.
26 Const P. VI, ch. 2, F [562].

this right (deliberately left vague, to avoid scruples) is defined in the Constitutions.[27]

The same copying error made the final words of the paragraph difficult to understand. In F40 the phrase read: "let them be content with what they are given out of charity for the necessities of life." "Out of charity," that is, "as alms," not as recompense for the work of apostolic ministries. This enshrines the norm that the professed must live on alms.[28] It does not say in so many words that the Society has both the use and the ownership of these things, given to it for the necessities of life, but this seems to be the most obvious interpretation.

II. THE EXCEPTION IN THE CASE OF THE SCHOLASTICS

Here too we can distinguish three sections or ideas: the purpose of the colleges, their temporal organization, the students received in the colleges.

1. The Purpose of the Colleges

"However, the houses which the Lord will provide are to be dedicated to labor in His vineyard and not to the pursuit of scholastic studies, and on the other hand it appears altogether proper that workers should be provided for that same vineyard from among the young men who are inclined to piety and capable of applying themselves to learning, in order that they may be a kind of seminary for the Society, including the professed Society."

This paragraph was not there at all in either F39 or F40. It was added in F50, although the ideas it contains are old, as we shall see presently.

It opens with a "however," as if to introduce an exception. It has often been said that there are two systems of poverty in the Society: that of the professed houses and that of the colleges. This division does not seem to respond to Ignatius' mind. He never speaks of the "poverty of the colleges," nor can colleges with revenues be said to be poor, even if the scholastics living in them are poor on account of their vow. Here, as well as in the Examen of the Constitutions,[29] the revenues of the colleges are presented as an exception in the matter of the Society's poverty, and

27 Const P. VI, ch. 2, n. 5, E, F [561-563].
28 Const P. VI, ch. 2, n. 3 [557].
29 Exam ch. 1, nn. 3 and 4 [4-5].

chapter 2 of Part VI, on "What pertains to poverty," mentions the colleges only to say that the professed and coadjutors should not ordinarily reside in them.[30]

The central idea of the paragraph is simple enough: it is good that young men be trained for the Society; since this cannot be done in the houses, we can have colleges to serve this purpose. The 1541 Constitutions contain the idea in embryo: "to open colleges in universities; neither studies nor lessons in the Society."[31]

It first mentions "the houses which the Lord will provide." These were later called "professed houses"; both here and in the Constitutions they are simply called "houses." They are houses of the Society because the colleges were regarded as institutions depending on the Society. The Lord is said to provide them because, in Ignatius' thinking, our benefactors are instruments of divine goodness.[32] These houses of the Society "are to be dedicated to labor in God's vineyard" (a reference to the parable of the laborers of the vineyard),[33] and not to have ecclesiastical studies in them. These studies, therefore, are not regarded as work in the Lord's vineyard but rather as a means to train laborers for the vineyard.

This is precisely the purpose of the colleges: to provide trained laborers for the vineyard. The idea had already been developed in a document dating back to the end of 1540 or beginning of 1541 under the title "Foundation of a College"[34] and was taken up in the Constitutions:[35] the Society cannot be preserved by taking only men already formed. Promising young men must be trained, for which colleges are needed.

Interestingly, these lines were written not for F39 or F40, but for F50, that is, when the Society had only one "house" properly so called but more than thirteen "colleges," most of which had started to give admission to outside students.

2. Administrative Organization of the Colleges

The greatest difference in this respect is not between F40 and F50 but between F39 and F40.

F39 did not as much as mention colleges. It just said: "However, for the purpose of keeping well-qualified students and educating them in universities, especially in the sacred sciences, they [the professed] may have

---

30 Const P. VI, ch. 2, nn. 3 and 4 [557, 560].
31 MI Const I 47.
32 Const P. IV, ch. 1, n. 1 [309].
33 Mt 20:1-16.
34 MI Const I 49-50, col. 1.
35 Const P. IV, preamble A [308].

civil right to stable goods and revenues for the support of such students." In other words, the professed may not own stable goods or revenues for the maintenance and use of the Society, but they may own them for the maintenance of students who attend a university.

The colleges come on the scene in F40. Not for the professed to own those stable goods and revenues; instead, there should be colleges close to universities and these colleges may own revenues and properties for the maintenance of the students.

We possess no historical documents to tell us how and why this change was effected. Ignatius once remarked to Gonçalves da Câmara that "it was Laínez who first hit on the idea" of the colleges.[36] But it is difficult to ascertain whether he referred to the creation of colleges or, in a wider sense, to the training of students in the universities. Indeed, the year that F40 was prepared (September 1539 to September 1540) Laínez was absent from Rome. The only significant difference between F40 and F50 concerns the places where these colleges ought to be located: not only in universities, but also elsewhere.

We can single out three ideas: establishment of the colleges, superintendency by the Society, advantages of this system.

a. Establishment of the Colleges

> "Consequently, to provide facilities for studies, the professed Society should be capable of having colleges of scholastics wherever benefactors will be moved by their devotion to build and endow them. We now petition that as soon as these colleges will have been built and endowed (but not from resources which it pertains to the Holy See to apply), they may be established through authorization of the Holy See or considered to be so established. These colleges should be capable of possessing fixed revenues, rights to rentals, or possessions which are to be applied to the uses and needs of the students."

These, then, are "colleges of scholastics," "to provide facilities for studies," on the model of the colleges of the university of Paris and other universities of the time, pious or charitable foundations for the benefit of poor students, to facilitate their studies in the university. But unlike them and unlike the colleges of F40, those of F50 can be established not only where there happens to be a university but also "wherever benefactors will

36 MI FontNarr I 610.

be moved by their devotion to build and endow them." The request is then made—and the pope grants this request by approving the Formula—that these colleges be considered papal foundations: "they may be established through authorization from the Holy See or considered to be so established." There is one exception: when the college is built and endowed "from resources which it pertains to the Holy See to apply," for in that case the Holy See's direct intervention is called for.

"The professed Society should be capable of having colleges" and "these colleges should be capable of possessing fixed revenues," etc. It no longer says, as F40 had, "the professed" but "the professed Society," presumably to indicate that it is not the professed taken individually but collectively. Nadal goes as far as saying that it is the professed together with the coadjutors.

The Latin verb "habere" is used with the double meaning of "having" and "owning" or "possessing": "the colleges should be capable of possessing fixed revenues, rights to rentals, or possessions." This was, in fact, Ignatius' opinion. In the above-mentioned "Foundation of a College" he stipulated that the founder should be made to agree to the college having dominion over its properties for the maintenance of the students and empowering it to receive moneys, properties, and revenues and to sue in court, if necessary, to preserve whatever belongs to it.[37] Later on, in an answer to Polanco, Ignatius declared: "as regards the colleges, the ownership should lie with the rector and the students."[38] So, then, when it is stated earlier that the Society "should be capable of having colleges," "having" cannot mean "possessing," but a relationship of dependence and utility. The matter was formally put by Ignatius to two Roman jurists in the following terms: "The bull states that our Society may have colleges with revenues. Does this include the dominion and ownership of the colleges (even though the use of revenues be restricted to the scholastics) or only the superintendency? In this latter case, who will have the ownership of the building and the revenues?" The answer of one of the jurists is obscure. The other one replied: "The college owns the revenues in common. The administration pertains to the superior general, and the dominion to the college."[39]

These revenues and properties "are to he applied to the uses and needs of the students," since it is for their sake that colleges are accepted, so that "workers may be provided for the Lord's vineyard," "to provide facilities for studies." They are "colleges of scholastics." Further on, the same idea

---

37 MI Const I 52.
38 *Dubiorum Series Quarta*, n. 41: MI Const I 327.
39 MI Const I 353.

is stressed in a negative way.

b. Superintendency by the Society

> "The general of the Society retains the full government or
> superintendency over the aforementioned colleges and
> students; and this pertains to the choice of the rectors or
> governors and of the scholastics; the admission, dismissal,
> reception, and exclusion of the same; the enactment of
> statutes; the arrangement, instruction, edification, and
> correction of the scholastics; the manner of supplying them
> with food, clothing, and all the other necessary materials;
> and every other kind of government, control, and care."

The principle is stated, and the extent of this superintendency is
declared.

The government or superintendency of these colleges is fully in the
hands of the superior general of the Society. This superintendency is not
mere supervision. It includes the government and administration of the
temporal goods.[40] It extends to whatever pertains to (1) the constitution of
the college ("choice of governors and scholastics, admission, dismissal, etc.");
(2) the norms governing the college ("enactment of statutes"); (3) the
formation of the scholastics (their "arrangement, instruction, etc."); (4) their
material support ("the manner of supplying them with food, clothing, etc.").
In short, all kind of "government, control, and care."

c. Advantages of This System

> "All this should be managed in such a way that neither may
> the students be able to abuse the aforementioned goods nor
> may the professed Society be able to convert them to its own
> uses, but may use them to provide for the needs of the
> scholastics."

This system offers two advantages: the students will not be able to
misuse these goods, because they will have the property and the use but
not the administration thereof, whereas the professed Society will have the
administration but not the use and so it will not be able to turn them to
its own use.

Ignatius wanted this to be understood honestly but without scruples. In

---

40 Const P. IV, ch. 2, C [327].

a reply to Polanco he indicated that, when joining a college, both rectors and scholastics should swear not to transfer to the Society the ownership of any stable goods or fixed revenues.[41] He used to do just this when a rector took office at the Roman College and the Germanicum. He even gave orders that no one from the house should go to either college for meals unless with special permission so that their rectors could take the oath with greater assurance that "the house had taken no advantage."[42] In order to avoid scruples in small matters, Polanco suggested the suppression of the negative sentence in the Formula: "nor may the professed Society be able to convert them to its own uses." Ignatius did not accept this suggestion; he preferred a declaration in the Constitutions to the effect that this directive should not be interpreted scrupulously. He agreed, however, to the canon lawyers' being consulted regarding the legitimacy of this interpretation.[43] This was done in the following terms: "The bull says that the Society must not use the revenues of the colleges for its own advantage. Does this exclude even small expenses, for instance, when the professed of the Society happen to stay in the college for a few days, or when they are helped with provisions for a journey or live in the college for an important reason, such as writing, taking into account that the mind of the founder of the Society is that such small expenditures should not be barred?" The jurists consulted replied in the affirmative,[44] and so it was declared in the Constitutions.[45]

3. The Students of the Colleges

> "These students, moreover, should have such intellectual ability and moral character as to give solid hope that they will be suitable for the Society's functions after their studies are completed, and that thus at length, after their progress in spirit and learning has become manifest and after sufficient testing, they can be admitted into our Society."

These are "colleges of scholastics," established "to provide facilities for studies." Who, then, are these students? F39 highlighted their intention of joining the Society: "those who wish to advance in spirit and learning and be eventually admitted when the course of their studies is over." F40 stressed the conditions necessary for granting them admission: the Society

41 *Dubiorum Series Quarta,* n. 41: MI Const I 327.
42 MI FontNarr I 560.
43 *Dubiorum Series Tertia:* MI Const I 308; *Series Quarta,* n. 45: ibid 328.
44 MI Const I 353.
45 Const P. IV, ch. 2, F [330]; P. VI, ch. 2, C [558].

should make sure of their progress and test them sufficiently. F50 added a few words about their qualities: enough intellectual ability and moral character so as to give solid hope that they will be suitable for the work of the Society.[46] They should not, therefore, be given admission except "after their progress in spirit and learning has become manifest and after sufficient testing." This is further explained in the Constitutions.[47]

46 Cf. Const P. IV, ch. 3, n. 2 [334].
47 Const P. V, ch. 2, nn. 1-2 [516-518].

THE FIFTH CHAPTER:
TWO JESUIT PECULIARITIES

Two topics are dealt with in this chapter of F50: choir, and common life in externals.

I. CHOIR

> "Since all the members should be priests, they should be obliged to recite the Divine Office according to the ordinary rite of the Church, but privately and not in common or in choir."

On this point F39 said, "All the members who are in holy orders, even though they can acquire no civil right to benefices and revenues, should nonetheless be obliged to recite the office according to the rite of the Church, but not in choir." F40 touched up a few expressions but kept the paragraph substantially unchanged.

The expression "the ordained members" is odd. It could be that it had not been made clear as yet that all the professed should be ordained priests. Polanco, who enquired if "all the professed should be priests," was told emphatically by Ignatius that they should.[1] Polanco noted likewise that the words "even though they may have no benefice" was superfluous because all priests are bound by common law to recite the office.[2] Hence the final wording: "Since all the members should be priests, they should be obliged to recite the Divine Office . . . , but privately and not in common or in choir."

This is one of the points of our Institute that has been criticized most, as though depriving the Society of something vital to religious life. Dom A. de Vogüé, O.S.B., has demonstrated that the Divine Office was part of the worship of each church and hence the responsibility of those who served

---

1 *Dubiorum Series Tertia:* MI Const I 310; *Series Quarta,* n. 52: ibid 329.
2 *Dubiorum Series Tertia:* MI Const I 310; *Series Quarta,* n. 49: ibid 329.

that church: canons, whether secular or regular. As far as the monks were concerned, the office was rather a peak moment in their prayer life, since the monk is supposed to be always in prayer.[3]

Ignatius, however, did not mean to forbid the choir in the Society: he only removed its obligation: "we remain free to have it when and where it may seem to contribute to God's greater service." This is what he told Polanco.[4] F39 gave this reason: that the Fathers "may not be prevented from performing the duties of charity to which we are fully committed." And it added: "Hence, too, they should not make use of music or singing in their Masses and other liturgical services. Other clerics and religious laudably use them to enhance divine worship and more effectively move the hearts of the people in tune with the hymns and the mysteries celebrated. But experience has shown us that they are an obstacle in our own case because, according to our vocation, we have to spend most of the day and even the night helping those who are physically or spiritually ill, in addition to all the other necessary duties."

This spells out the specific character of the Jesuit vocation: though priestly, it is not primarily connected with worship but rather prophetic, its aim being evangelization, not divine worship.

All this was removed in F40, yielding to Cardinal Ghinucci's objections. He feared that it might confirm the ideas of the Lutherans in their opposition to Catholic worship.[5]

II. COMMON LIFE IN MATTERS EXTERNAL

> "Also, in what pertains to food, clothing, and other external things, they will follow the common and approved usage of reputable priests, so that if anything is subtracted in this regard in accordance with each one's need or desire of spiritual progress, it may be offered, as will be fitting, out of devotion and not obligation, as a reasonable service of the body to God."

---

3 Cf. A. de Vogüé, O.S.B., "Le sens de l'Office divin d'après la Règle de S. Benoît," in *Revue d'Ascétique et Mystique* 42 (1966), 389-404.
4 *Dubiorum Series Tertia*: MI Const I 310; *Series Quarta*, n. 51: ibid 329.
5 Cf. F. Dittrich, *Regesten und Briefe des Cardinals Gaspare Contarini* (Braunsberg 1881), 379.

F39 had another paragraph, likewise dropped in F40 for a similar reason. This paragraph warned future Jesuits lest they should, under the appearance of good, "impose under pain of mortal sin any fasts, disciplines, baring of feet or head, color of dress, type of food, penances, hairshirts, and other torments of the flesh." "We forbid them, not indeed because we are against such things (in fact we praise and admire those who practice them), but solely because we do not want Ours to be oppressed under so many labors and pretend that this excuses them from performing the tasks to which we are committed. Each one, however, may out of devotion, with the superior's approval, practice what he thinks necessary or helpful to himself." Later on these ideas found their way into the Examen of the Constitutions.[6]

When F50 was being prepared, Polanco asked if it would be good to say a word about clothing and other externals. Ignatius replied that it could be stated in general terms that food and clothing should follow the common usage of reputable priests.[7] This is what we now read in the Formula. It states the norm and suggests its advantages.

The norm is that "in what pertains to food, clothing, and other external things, they will follow the common and approved usage of exemplary priests." I prefer the word "exemplary"; "honesti" are the priests who observe the "honestas clericalis," those who observe the norms.[8]

"What pertains to food, clothing, and other external things" covers all that was said in F39: clothing, fasts and abstinence, and other penances and austerities. The members of the Society should not have a usage of their own in all this but should follow the common and ordinary custom. Not that of the laity, but of good and reputable or exemplary secular priests. And not any usage, but the one that has the approval of competent ecclesiastical authority.

The advantage of this norm is that, in this way, "if anything is subtracted in this regard [i.e., in the matter of fasts, etc.] in accordance with each one's need or desire of spiritual progress, it may be offered, as will be fitting, out of devotion and not obligation, as a reasonable service of the body to God." These last words echo those of Romans 12:1: "Think of God's mercy, my brothers, and worship Him, I beg you, in a way that is worthy of human beings, by offering your living bodies as a holy sacrifice, truly pleasing, to God."

---

6 Exam ch. 1, n. 6 [8].
7 *Dubiorum Series Tertia:* MI Const I 310; *Series Quarta*, n. 68: ibid 333.
8 Cf. M. Dortel-Claudot, *Le genre de vie extérieure de la Compagnie de Jésus* (Rome 1971).

From all that has been said, one deduces that the norm "common usage of exemplary priests" is not a norm of poverty, as has sometimes been thought, but a norm referring to austerity of life.

THE CONCLUDING REMARKS

The last paragraphs form the conclusion. After a reference to the purpose of the Formula, a warning to future Jesuits follows, urging them not to admit anyone who does not meet the requirements, to profession or even to the vows of coadjutors or scholastics. A prayer and a doxology bring the Formula to an end.

I. PURPOSE OF THE FORMULA

> "These are the matters which we were able to explain about our profession in a kind of sketch, through the good pleasure of our previously mentioned sovereign pontiff Paul and of the Apostolic See. We have now completed this explanation, in order to give brief information both to those who ask us about our plan of life and also to those who will later follow us if, God willing, we shall ever have imitators along this path."

The Formula is an explanation of their profession offered by Ignatius and his companions "in a kind of sketch."

The word "profession" occurs rather often in Ignatian writings; it signifies the kind of life we profess, the manner of imitating Christ proper to our vocation. The word "sketch" translates the Latin word "typus," which actually means a bas-relief figure. The Formula, then, according to its authors, is meant to present a picture of the Society's kind of life. That is why GC 31 (1966) says that "the Formula sets forth the fundamental structure of the Society."[1] This is submitted to "the good pleasure" of the reigning pontiff and of the Apostolic See, the competent authority to approve religious orders.

---

1 GC 31, d. 4, n. 3.

The purpose in presenting this picture of the Society is "to give brief information both to those who ask us about our plan of life and also to those who will later follow us," that is—they add with humility and confidence in God—"if, God willing, we shall ever have imitators along this path," in "this Institute which is, so to speak, a pathway to God."

God willed that they should have followers. These followers, then, ought to listen to these words as though addressed to them and recognize in this Formula the authentic image of the Society of Jesus.

II. CAUTION IN ADMITTING TO PROFESSION

> "By experience we have learned that the path has many and great difficulties connected with it. Consequently we have judged it opportune to decree that no one should be permitted to pronounce his profession in this Society unless his life and doctrine have been probed by long and exacting tests (as will be explained in the Constitutions). For in all truth this Institute requires men who are thoroughly humble and prudent in Christ as well as conspicuous in the integrity of Christian life and learning."

At this point F39 contained two warnings to future Jesuits. The first, concerning the imposition by rule of bodily austerities, has already been dealt with in chapter 5; it was suppressed in deference to the scruples of Cardinal Ghinucci. The second advised caution in admitting to profession. The reason for both warnings was that Ignatius and his companions knew from experience that this path or way of life "has many and great difficulties." The document "Foundation of a College" said graphically: "One who enters a well-ordered monastery will be farther away from occasions of sin than in our Society on account of the stricter enclosure and greater peace and order. Our Society does not have that enclosure, quiet, and peace, but goes about from one place to another. Furthermore, one who has had bad habits and lacks perfection has every chance for perfection in a monastery so ordered. It is otherwise in our Society; a candidate must be well tested and tried before admission because after admission he will have to go about and deal with all sorts of people, both men and women, and such dealings require greater strength and greater testing, and greater graces and gifts from our Creator and Lord."[2]

2 MI Const I 60.

The difficulties of this way of life make it imperative that only persons who are well known and well chosen be admitted to profession.

Well known: "probed by long and exacting tests" both as regards life and doctrine. The professed must be such that he can be trusted on both counts and recommended to the pope. This cannot be achieved unless he is submitted to protracted and demanding tests. The Constitutions speak of these tests mainly in the Examen and in Part V.[3]

Well chosen: "for in all truth this Institute requires men who are thoroughly humble and prudent in Christ." F39 read: "Only when he appears prudent in Christ and conspicuous either in learning or in holiness of life may he be admitted into the militia of Jesus Christ." F40 changed "holiness of life" into "purity of Christian life." The expression "conspicuous in holiness" must have seemed inappropriate.

Polanco found the word "conspicuous" objectionable, as smacking of arrogance. Ignatius suggested "the following general approach: they should remember that the Institute of the Society requires persons who are humble and prudent in Christ, and eminent in learning, or well versed in it, etc."[4] We saw that this was done in F50.

The word "humble" was added in his own hand by Ignatius[5] and shows the interior and exterior attitude of submission and service that must characterize the Jesuit "in conformity with our profession of humility and lowliness."[6]

"Prudent in Christ." The Lord sent the Apostles "like sheep among wolves" and taught them to be both prudent and simple.[7] Prudence, to be sure, but prudence "in Christ," geared to Christ's service and glory, based on his teachings, enlightened by his grace. Not a "prudence according to the flesh,"[8] nor the Machiavellian craftiness of which Jesuits have so often, rightly or wrongly, been accused.

"Conspicuous" is something that draws people's eyes and attention. Not that all the professed must possess an eminent or extraordinary degree of virtue and learning. It is rather a question of the credibility and moral authority that result from a blameless life and good theological formation.

It is worth noting that, in its final draft, the Formula demands that the professed be eminent in both: "in the integrity of Christian life and learning." The previous draft had "either in learning or in holiness of life."

---

3 Exam ch. 4, nn. 9-28 [64-83]; Const P V, ch. 1, nn. 2-3 [512-514].
4 *Dubiorum Series Tertia:* MI Const I 310; *Series Quarta,* n. 54: 330.
5 *Dubiorum Series Quarta,* n. 54: 330.
6 Const P. X, n. 6 [817].
7 Mt 10:16.
8 Cf. Rom 8:6.

In fact, at the beginning, not all the professed were required to be learned. The 1539 resolution of the first Fathers to vow obedience to the pope spoke of those who "have sufficiency" and those who are "less sufficient."[9] In their 1541 meeting the Fathers decided that the "learned" (those with university degrees) should be more numerous than those not learned, at least two thirds of the total, and that the lack of learning should be made up for with other natural or supernatural qualities which would give them credibility and moral authority.

Experience must have taught Ignatius that the pope's "missions" required men with a solid theological formation. He told Polanco, who asked him whether all the professed should be "learned," that they certainly should, and he added: "but this sufficiency in learning may be understood somewhat broadly."[10]

What did Ignatius understand by "conspicuous in learning"? We have heard him speak of "sufficiency" and that, too, understood broadly, not rigidly. The same concept comes up in the Constitutions: "such persons should have sufficient learning."[11] "Sufficient," however, is a relative term: sufficient for what? The Ignatian documents have this unanimous answer: for the ministries of the Society. A report about the Society addressed to Charles V, for instance, stated that only "well-screened and learned persons, with talent for preaching and hearing confessions" were given admission.[12] And an old resolution read: those to be accepted must be learned, "having a fair sufficiency to preach and hear confessions."[13] It is not required that they be luminaries, but they should have the intellectual preparation and authority required for "the function of sowing the divine word."[14]

III. THE COADJUTORS

This paragraph is new. F39 and F40 did not have it, obviously because the coadjutors were introduced in the Institute later on through the brief "Exponi nobis" of 1546. When F50 was being prepared, Polanco asked Ignatius whether anything should be said about the coadjutors. The founder replied that something should be said but without going into detail

---

9 MI Const I 47-48, nn. 46-48.
10 *Dubiorum Series Tertia:* MI Const I 310; *Series Quarta:* ibid. n. 53, 330.
11 Const P. V, ch. 2, n. 2 [518].
12 MI Const I 242.
13 Ibid 212; Cf. Const P. IV, preamble, A [308].
14 Exam ch. 2, n. 6 [30]; ch. 5, n. 6 [109].

nor mentioning their qualities, indicating only that they should be fit, so as not to cause delays in the approval of the Formula.[15]

So it was done. It was added right at the end, in connection with the "long and exacting tests." The idea of coadjutors was a novel element, peculiar to the Society, with nothing like it in any other religious order. Ignatius may have feared that, when it came to drafting the bull, this point, even though already approved by the pope, would raise the same kind of difficulties caused earlier by other points of our Institute.

Two topics are touched on: care to admit as coadjutors only those who are fit, and the kind of vows they are to take. The original Latin text mentions this second point in a parenthesis embedded in the main sentence, which deals with the first point.[16]

1. *Fitness*

> "Moreover, some persons will be admitted to become coadjutors, either for spiritual or temporal concerns, or to become scholastics. . . . These coadjutors and scholastics too should be admitted into this militia of Jesus Christ only after they have been diligently examined and found suitable for that same end of the Society."

This is the only passage of the Formula dealing with those who "will be admitted to become coadjutors either for spiritual or temporal concerns." The 1546 brief approving this grade describes them as priests who help the professed in spiritual matters or ministries and laymen who help them in temporal matters and domestic tasks. This description is explained in greater detail in the Constitutions.[17]

The scholastics too are mentioned. But I suspect this is a parenthesis, added at a later stage, because the Formula had already spoken of the scholastics and the fitness required for their admission.

No one should be admitted until he has been "diligently examined and found suitable for that same end." All must cooperate towards the end described in the first chapter, each though "according to the particular grade of his own vocation." Laínez explained this diversity by comparing it to that of the builders of a church: some, for instance, work as master

---

15 *Dubiorum Series Tertia:* MI Const I 313; *Series Quarta*, n. 62: 331.
16 This "sandwiching" of the second point in the first is reflected in the English translation [editor's note].
17 Exam ch. 6, nn. 1-2 [112-114].

masons or principal builders (the professed), others as their helpers (the coadjutors), yet others as apprentices (the scholastics).[18]

The Constitutions will explain what qualities the coadjutors must have in order to be considered fit.[19]

2. The Vows

> "After sufficient probations and the time specified in the Constitutions, these too should, for their greater devotion and merit, pronounce their vows. But their vows will not be solemn (except in the case of some who with permission from the superior general will be able to make three solemn vows of this kind because of their devotion and personal worth). Instead, they will be vows by which these persons are bound as long as the superior general thinks that they should be retained in the Society, as will be explained more fully in the Constitutions."

"These too should . . . pronounce their vows": who are "these"? The official Latin text reads "utrique," literally "the former and the latter." But who are "the former and the latter"? The coadjutors and the scholastics, or the spiritual and temporal coadjutors? The former interpretation is the more obvious and has been followed by Nadal and other authors. But I have already mentioned that the word "scholastics" may have been added to the text at a later stage. If the Latin "utrique" referred to both coadjutors and scholastics we would have to conclude, with Nadal, that the scholastics too may take solemn vows while remaining in the grade of approved scholastics, which is, I think, unacceptable. When F50 was prepared and approved, only the vow of joining the Society was prescribed for the scholastics. The three vows of poverty, chastity, and obedience were added in a correction made in the definitive text of the Constitutions, towards 1552-1553.[20] Could the vow to enter the Society as a professed or a coadjutor be solemn?

Part VI of the Constitutions establishes the time for admission to vows.[21] When directing that, after the year of noviceship, the novice should be either promoted to profession or dismissed, the Council of Trent made

---

18 Cf. C. de Dalmases, "Le esortazioni del P. Laínez sull'Examen Constitutionum" in AHSI 35 (1966) 151.

19 Const P. V, ch. 2, n. 4 [522].

20 Cf. E. Olivares, *Los votos de los escolares de la Compañía de Jesús, su evolución jurídica* (Rome 1961) 25-28.

21 Const P V, ch. 1, n. 3, C [514-515].

an exception in favor of the Society and that was when it approved its Institute, calling it "pious and holy."[22]

The coadjutors should pronounce their vows "for their greater devotion and merit." These are the same words we read in the brief "Exponi nobis" and in the aide-memoire handed over by Ignatius to the cardinal who had to discuss the matter with the pope.[23] At the beginning Ignatius wondered about the juridical modalities of this new institution and even whether it was necessary at all that these helpers of the professed should take vows.[24]

Next the nature of the vows is determined: they are not solemn, and they will bind "as long as the superior general thinks that they should be retained in the Society—as will be explained more fully in the Constitutions." The Constitutions declare these vows to be simple and taken with a tacit condition, namely, "if the Society will desire to retain them."[25]

But there may be exceptions. The superior general may allow some "to make three solemn vows of this kind because of their devotion and personal worth." This is the first time these three solemn vows are mentioned; none of the earlier documents had mentioned them.

It should be noted that this exception regards the vows of coadjutors, not of the professed. As Nadal points out, those who make these vows are coadjutors of solemn vows, not professed who have not taken the fourth vow. On the other hand, the text makes no distinction between spiritual and temporal coadjutors. We know of at least one temporal coadjutor with solemn vows in Ignatius' time. He took them in order to annul his former marriage.[26] The Constitutions, however, imply that those who take these three solemn vows are priests—indeed, that they are professed who do not have the fourth vow rather than coadjutors with solemn vows.[27]

IV. PRAYER AND DOXOLOGY

"And may Christ deign to be favorable to these our tender beginnings, to the glory of God the Father, to whom alone be glory and honor forever. Amen."

22 Council of Trent, 25th session, "De regularibus," ch. 16.
23 Cf. J. M. March, "Documentos insignes que pertenecieron al cardenal Zelada, tocantes a la Compañía de Jesús," in AHSI 18 (1949) 123.
24 Ibid.
25 Const P. V, ch. 4, B [536].
26 Bro. Diego de Avila in 1555. Cf. M. Scaduto, *Catalogo dei gesuiti d'Italia 1540-1565* (Rome 1968) 8-9.
27 Const P. V, ch. 2, n. 3, C [520-521].

The Formula concludes with a prayer to Christ that he may deign to favor these "weak attempts," "weak beginnings" ("tenuia incepta"), gearing it all "to the glory of God the Father." The final doxology is based on those used by St. Paul.[28]

28 Cf. Rom 16:27; 1 Tim 1:17, 6:16.

FINAL REFLECTIONS

The picture of the Society that emerges from the Formula of the Institute coincides with the one traced out by Pope Paul VI in his address of 3 December 1974: the Society of Jesus is a religious, priestly, and apostolic order, united to the Roman pontiff by a special bond of love and service.

I. A PRIESTLY RELIGIOUS ORDER

The Society is formed of priests who desire to serve in it as soldiers of God under the banner of the Cross and to serve the Lord alone and the Church his Spouse under the Roman pontiff, the vicar of Christ on earth; they pronounce a solemn vow of chastity, poverty, and obedience; they have helpers or coadjutors whose vows (except for some cases) are not solemn though they are binding "as long as the superior general thinks that they should be retained in the Society"; they likewise have colleges for young scholastics, who may be admitted into the Society after they have completed their studies. These colleges form a kind of seminary for the Society.

Because it is a religious order, it has a superior general, "elected by a majority of votes," who shall "possess all the authority and power over the Society which are useful for its good administration, correction, and government," with "full right personally to order and command whatever he judges in the Lord to pertain to the glory of God and the common good"; "the decision about each one's grade and the selection and distribution of employments" shall also be in his power. The Society has laws, too: Constitutions which help towards the achievement of its aim. It has a chapter or general congregation, as a council for the general, "which must necessarily be convoked to establish or change the Constitutions and for other matters of more than ordinary importance"; this council is to be constituted by "the greater part of the Society which can be summoned without grave inconvenience by the superior general," "with the majority of votes always having the right to prevail."

II. AN APOSTOLIC ORDER

The Society has been "founded chiefly for this purpose: to strive especially for the defense and propagation of the faith and for the progress of souls in Christian life and doctrine, by means of public preaching, lectures, and any other ministration whatsoever of the word of God, and further by means of the Spiritual Exercises, the education of children and unlettered persons in Christianity, and the spiritual consolation of Christ's faithful through hearing confessions and administering the other sacraments." But the members of the Society should also be ready "to reconcile the estranged, compassionately assist and serve those who are in prisons or hospitals, and indeed to perform any other works of charity, according to what will seem expedient for the glory of God and the common good."

This life of evangelizaton life must be lived out in "evangelical poverty," the poverty Christ taught to the Apostles when he sent them to preach. In conformity with that, "all these works should be carried out altogether free of charge"; "neither the professed, either as individuals or in common, nor any house or church of theirs can acquire any civil right to any produce, fixed revenues, or possessions or to the retention of any stable goods (except those which are proper for their own use and habitation), but they should instead be content with whatever is given them out of charity for the necessities of life." Even though the Society may have colleges of scholastics "to provide facilities for studies," and these colleges may possess fixed revenues, incomes, and properties, all administered by the Society, yet the Society cannot "convert them to its own uses" but only use them "to provide for the needs of the scholastics."

On account also of the demands of this apostolic life, the members of the Society will not be obliged to recite the Divine Office in common or in choir, and "in what pertains to food, clothing, and other external things, they will follow the common and approved usage of reputable priests."

Likewise, "the houses which the Lord will provide are to be dedicated to labor in His vineyard and not to the pursuit of scholastic studies." However, for the purpose of training future workers for the Lord's vineyard, the Society may have colleges of young scholastics under its supervision.

III. AN ORDER UNITED BY A SPECIAL BOND TO THE POPE

"This entire Society and the individual members who make their profession in it are campaigning for God under faithful obedience to His Holiness" the pope. Hence, in addition to the ordinary bond of the three "religious vows," the professed are obliged "by a special vow to carry out, without subterfuge or excuse and at once (as far as in us lies), whatever the present and future Roman pontiffs may order pertaining to the progress of souls and the propagation of the faith, and to go to whatsoever provinces they may choose to send us, among the Turks or any other infidels, even those who live in the regions called the Indies, or among any heretics or schismatics or any of the faithful."

"This path" (or way of life) "has many and great difficulties"; it "requires men who are thoroughly humble and prudent in Christ, as well as conspicuous in the integrity of Christian life and learning." "Therefore, before those who will come to us take this burden upon their shoulders, they should ponder long and seriously whether they possess among their resources enough spiritual capital to complete this tower." After they join the Society, they must not be admitted to profession until their life and doctrine have been "probed by long and exacting tests." Even those accepted as spiritual and temporal coadjutors or as scholastics should be "admitted into this militia of Jesus Christ only after they have been diligently examined and found suitable for that same end of the Society."

* * *

The Formula of the Institute is not merely a juridical document. It contains valuable teachings on the spiritual life. I should like to point out some.

The Institute of the Society is "a pathway to God" one must walk with ardent zeal, spiritual discretion, and humility and abnegation.

With ardent zeal.—The candidate is urged to "strive with all his effort to achieve this end set before him by God," "prompt in carrying out this obligation which is so great, being clad for battle day and night."

With spiritual discretion.—Even before committing himself, he should ponder whether the Holy Spirit is offering him so much grace that he can hope to bear the weight of his vocation, and then he must strive to achieve the end of the Society "according to the grace which the Holy Spirit has given to him and according to the particular grade of his own vocation." That is why the Institute of the Society requires men who are "prudent in

Christ." Lest anyone be moved by indiscreet zeal, "the decision about each one's grade and the selection and distribution of employments shall be in the power of the superior general," who "should issue the commands which he knows to be opportune for achieving the end set before him by God and the Society." Furthermore, one of the reasons for making the vow of obedience to the pope is to have a "surer direction from the Holy Spirit."

With humility and abnegation—with complete surrender to God. Still another reason for the vow of obedience to the pope is a "greater abnegation of our own wills." A good deal of abnegation is certainly required to carry out immediately, without subterfuge or excuse, whatever the pope may order concerning the progress of souls and the propagation of the faith, and to go to whatsoever provinces he may choose to send us, suppressing any ambition or any refusal of such missions or provinces, and leaving all this care to God, the pope himself, and the superior general. Likewise, one of the reasons for being obedient to the superior is "the constant practice of humility, never sufficiently praised." That is why "this Institute requires men who are thoroughly humble." Poverty too is entirely founded on detachment from temporal goods and full surrender to and confidence in God. The first Fathers had the spiritual experience that "a life removed as far as possible from all contagion of avarice and as like as possible to evangelical poverty is more gratifying, more undefiled, and more suitable for the edification of our fellowmen" and that "our Lord Jesus Christ supplies to his servants who seek only the kingdom of God what is necessary for food and clothing."

The compass and guide for this path is Christ the Lord, who pervades everything in the Formula, from beginning to end. The Society asks to be designated by His name. The Formula is proposed to "whoever desires to serve as a soldier of God beneath the banner of the Cross and to serve the Lord alone and the Church" inasmuch as she is his Spouse and under His vicar on earth. Such a one is urged to keep before his eyes, as long as he lives, first of all God and then the nature of this Institute; but, because the Institute is "a pathway to God," it is in reality not just a pathway by which the Jesuit goes to God, but also one by which he brings others to Him.

The pope is seen as the vicar of Christ, the one who takes his place on earth. Christ must be recognized and reverenced as present in the superior of the Society. The superior himself must be ever mindful of the kindness, meekness, and charity of Christ, whom he represents.

Finally, the Formula concludes with a humble prayer to Christ, to favor these modest beginnings and gear them to the glory of God the Father, to whom all praise and honor is ultimately directed.

INDEX OF NAMES

Avila, Brother Diego de, 101
Badía, Tommaso, 30
Beltrán of Loyola, 30
Benedict, St., 34, 37, 38, 73
Bonaventure, St., 35
Borgia, St. Francis, S.J., 32
Caraffa, Cardinal Gian Pietro, 77
Carpi, Cardinal Pio di, 31
Charles V, King, 98
Constantinus ab Aldeaseca,
    O.M.Cap., 78
Contarini, Cardinal Gaspare, 30,
    31, 92
Dalmases, Cándido de, S.J., 38,
    100
Dittrich, F., 30, 92
Dominic, St., 35, 38, 78
Dortel-Claudot, Michel, S.J., 90
Estrada, Antonio, S.J., 79
Favre, Pierre (Faber, Peter), 28,
    29, 56, 59
Francis, St., 32, 33, 35, 38, 78
Ghinucci, Cardinal Girolamo, 30,
    31, 57, 92, 96
Gonçalves da Câmara, Luis, S.J.,
    85
Gregory the Great, Pope St., 70
Guidiccioni, Cardinal Bartolomeo,
    31
Horace (Q. Horatius Flaccus), 63
Ignatius of Loyola, St., 25-28, 30-
    33, 37-39, 41, 43, 45-47, 49,
    50, 52-54, 57, 59, 61, 63-65,
    68, 69, 71, 72, 75, 76-78, 80,
    82-88, 91-93, 95-99, 101

Iturrioz, Jesús, S.J., 49, 67
Joseph, St., 38
Julius III, Pope, 33, 34
Laínez, Diego, S.J., 29, 30, 38, 41,
    85, 99, 100
Mainardi, Agostino, 41
Mariana, Juan, S.J., 53
Mendizábal, Luis, S.J., 67, 73
Morano, Matthew Sebastian de, 63
Nadal, Jerónimo, S.J., 25, 26, 30,
    37, 43, 44, 60, 65, 70, 86, 100,
    101
Olivares, Estanislao, S.J., 100
Paul III, Pope, 6-7, 19, 27, 30, 48,
    52, 55-58, 102,
Paul VI, Pope, 49, 103
Paul, St., 12-13, 38, 70, 95
Peter, St., 12-13, 28, 29, 70, 72
Pius VII, Pope, 33
Polanco, Juan Alfonso de, S.J., 27,
    30, 32, 38, 39, 41, 43-45, 49,
    52-54, 57, 60, 61, 64, 65, 68,
    69, 71, 82, 86-88, 91, 92, 93,
    97, 98
Pozzo, Giacomo del, 41
Ribadeneira, Pedro de, S.J., 70
Rodrigues, Simão, S.J., 27, 41
Salagnac, Etienne de, 38
Salmerón, Alfonso, S.J., 30
Scaduto, Mario, S.J., 101
Schurhammer, Georg, S.J., 79, 80
Tacchi Venturi, Pietro, S.J., 33, 41
Verdolay, Juan, 28
Vogüé, Adalbert de, O.S.B., 91, 92
Zelada, Cardinal, 101